open-plan living

open-plan
living

CYNTHIA INIONS

photography by ANDREW WOOD

RYLAND
PETERS
& SMALL

LONDON NEW YORK

For this edition:
Designer Sarah Rock
Commissioning editor Annabel Morgan
Production Patricia Harrington
Location research Kate Brunt and Nadine Bazar
Publishing director Alison Starling

Stylist Cynthia Inions
Plans Russell Bell

First published in the United Kingdom in 1999 by
Ryland Peters & Small as *One Space Living*.
This new compact edition published in 2007
by Ryland Peters & Small
20–21 Jockey's Fields
London WC1R 4BW
10 9 8 7 6 5 4 3

ISBN: 978-1-84597-556-2

A CIP record for this book is available from
the British Library

Printed and bound in China

contents

introduction

For more and more people, a single-space home is the solution to the challenge of contemporary living. Open-plan living offers the freedom to organize the home to suit the new informality in the way we live and spend time with our family and friends, the diversity of fast-paced modern lifestyles and the demand for a multi-functional environment.

Designing and planning an open-plan living environment from scratch, or simply revising a conventional interior, presents an opportunity to use the available space more efficiently and imaginatively, to create a welcoming and flexible home environment and enjoy a new sense of light, openness and integration. Introducing permanent partitions or reconfiguring space with flexible dividers can provide a comfortable and essential degree of separation between public and private areas without compromising the unity or versatility of the space.

The open-plan home utilizes a new and dynamic vocabulary of space, light and freedom of choice. This book presents an inspiring and individual collection of many different open-plan environments, from radical conversions of industrial buildings to simple low-level reworkings of typical domestic spaces, from cutting-edge concrete and glass constructions to family-friendly environments abundant with colour and comfort.

opposite A dynamic conversion of a post-office sorting depot provides a versatile split-level open-plan interior. **above left** Flip-up and pull-down panels can expose and enclose different elements of this kitchen area as desired. **above right** In a two-level loft, knocking through from one floor level to another radically improves the light distribution and sense of openness.

open-plan
living

why open-plan? I options I help

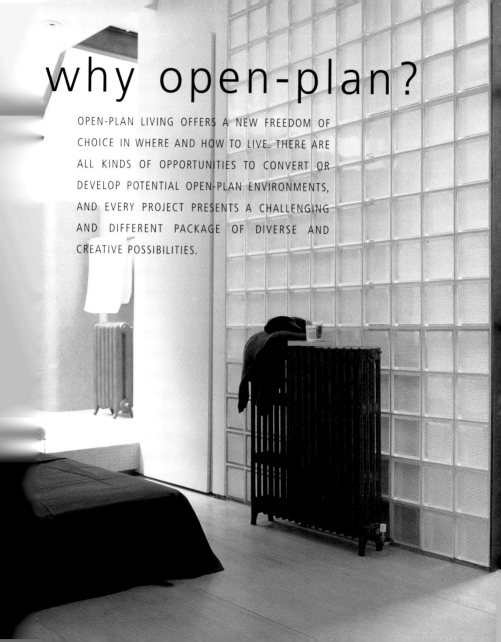

why open-plan?

OPEN-PLAN LIVING OFFERS A NEW FREEDOM OF
CHOICE IN WHERE AND HOW TO LIVE. THERE ARE
ALL KINDS OF OPPORTUNITIES TO CONVERT OR
DEVELOP POTENTIAL OPEN-PLAN ENVIRONMENTS,
AND EVERY PROJECT PRESENTS A CHALLENGING
AND DIFFERENT PACKAGE OF DIVERSE AND
CREATIVE POSSIBILITIES.

Freedom

In an open-plan environment, everything is up for review. Conventional ideas about designing and planning a domestic interior are irrelevant – in an open-plan home, there is no need to separate and confine everyday activities within a restrictive traditional layout. Whether you reconfigure a conventional space, take on an existing open-plan scheme and adapt it, or convert a previously non-domestic unit, the design and planning decisions will always be specific to every project.

Of all the possibilities, converting or refitting a non-domestic environment offers the maximum creative freedom. It allows you to develop an original space, removed from any references to domestic architectural proportions, structures and materials. Alternatively, stripping a domestic interior to an empty shell and beginning again can be an equally exciting undertaking. Nevertheless, it's important to be aware that projects like these are expensive undertakings that require a great deal of commitment, time, and energy.

Less ambitious schemes offer varying degrees of creative freedom. Sometimes an existing interior can be modified and improved by opening up the space. Introducing uniform floor coverings or lighting systems throughout can bring a new sense of integration and harmony and create the impression of spacious open-plan living without requiring massive disruption or expense.

left The raw architecture of a former printworks provided an inspiring starting point for this new domestic scheme. Visible metal support beams, concrete paving-slab flooring and heavy-duty professional catering equipment are in keeping with the industrial aesthetic of the space.

OPEN-PLAN LIVING OFFERS AN OPPORTUNITY TO MAKE THE MOST OF YOUR AVAILABLE SPACE

Sense of space

above left and opposite In a loft conversion, removing part of an upper floor and adding a double-height window optimizes light and space.
above centre The mezzanine level provides a series of areas for relaxing, sleeping, bathing and working. Sliding panels make flexible dividers.
above right The sleek, minimalist kitchen area is kept deliberately free of clutter, adding to the overall sense of space and light.

A sense of space is life-enhancing and makes all the difference between a dynamic, welcoming environment and an unappealing one. Open-plan living offers the opportunity to make the most of your space, whatever its size or shape.

There are many different ways to create or increase a sense of space, from large-impact structural alterations to a simple process of paring down and elimination. Radical transformations, like removing walls or floors to create a double-height space, increasing the size of windows or converting redundant roof space, will all increase a feeling of openness and improve light distribution

However, maximum openness is not always the best way forward. In conventional interiors, it is not always possible to remove internal walls, either

for structural reasons or because imposing a radical open-plan layout will spoil the overall proportions of the space. If this is the case, reducing the size of walls, either vertically or horizontally, adding portholes or creating internal windows will all provide a degree of openness and sense of connection while preserving original divisions and supports.

Reorganization on a smaller scale can also help to increase the perception of space. Getting rid of excess furniture and clutter is an effective and immediate way to increase space. For example, only allow sufficient chairs around a table, and store any surplus. Keep kitchen surfaces clear and stack magazines and books in storage systems. Everything, no matter how appealing or valuable, takes up space, so subtract anything unnecessary or excessive and see the difference.

opposite In an industrial conversion, lightweight paper screens are used to define and separate different areas. The screens can move to suit changing needs.

left and below Precise planning and high spec details, like this folding, curving screen, provide maximum flexibility in a tiny townhouse conversion.

Flexibility

Open-plan living has potential for maximum flexibility, allowing you to optimize space. The traditional Japanese interior demonstrates how to manipulate space to suit different activities by using panels or screens to sub-divide a single unit into different configurations. This principle of dividing a space to provide degrees of separation and privacy without compromising a sense of unity is a good model for contemporary environments.

Paper blinds, freestanding screens and fabric dividers all work effectively as low-cost, temporary fittings. For example, a bath in an open-plan bedroom gains privacy when screened with a length of fabric, while an apartment can be sub-divided into separate living and work areas by ceiling-to-floor lengths of paper hanging from hooks. Architectural devices such as transparent or solid panels, rotating sections of wall and doors that fold out, slide across or swing into place as partitions are also ingenious solutions, although such divisions are more permanent. For true flexibility, provide options for both openness and enclosure, thus meeting your changing needs without committing to a permanent configuration of your space.

FLEXIBILITY IS AN ESSENTIAL ELEMENT OF OPEN-PLAN LIVING

Integration

Open-plan living allows you to create a multi-functional living environment that will meet all your needs. By grouping activities into zones, you can create an efficient and enjoyable place in which to live. Yet different activities tend to overlap, so working out how best to combine different activities within zones and how to integrate zones within a single space is a complex issue.

Before making any decisions about integration, first consider the multitude of routine activities that take place in your home. Group any related activities together in one zone, or in zones that are in close proximity to each other. Position the zones according to frequency of use, ease of access and proximity to other zones. Consider the progression from public to private zones, and install flexible dividers or incorporate an intermediate cross-over area between the two.

The main challenge of integration is maintaining an intrinsic quality of openness in an interior while still making

adequate provision for privacy and reclusion. Striking this balance is a key factor in determining how comfortable it is to live in an open-plan home, especially if you are part of a busy family unit with people of all ages sharing the same space. Be aware of the day-to-day demands on your space and use dividers to screen more intimate zones, such as bathing or sleeping areas.

Often, the ideal solution is a reconciliation of what is practical, logical and cost-efficient. Special architectural or structural features might perhaps pre-designate an area for one specific use or suggest the arrangement of a sequence of zones. The position of utilities and drains, for example, will indicate possible locations for kitchen sinks and baths. Even so, with resourceful planning and possible re-routing of service systems, it is always possible to avoid over-compartmentalizing activities in a conventional way. After all, freedom, flexibility and individual expression are the whole point of open-plan living.

opposite left
Integrating a bathing and sitting area is an unconventional arrangement. However, the orientation of this salvaged bath and sofa adds a degree of separation.
left Widening the existing openings, removing doors and reducing the height of internal walls are all simple, low-key ways of improving integration between formerly separate areas in conventional domestic interiors.

this page Simple white roller blinds diffuse incoming light from full-width windows, changing the emphasis from the external to the internal environment.
opposite At a bay window, floor-to-ceiling roller blinds add an essential element of privacy and separation from the busy street outside without reducing light levels.

Positive assets

Converting an interior into a single space means that positive
assets, such as ample daylight or a great view, are accessible
throughout the space, not exclusive to one part of it.

Light enlivens and enhances everything: a plain white wall,
the colour and texture of fabric, the shape and line of furniture.
It does not simply provide illumination, but is a vital asset that
can animate a space with contrast and variation. Mapping out
the direction from which light enters a space and moves around
it is essential when planning structural changes to increase the
amount of light in an interior or improve its distribution. This
information will help you plan your space to make the most of
the available light at different times of day. You may wish to
position a sleeping area so you wake up to sunlight, or site a
work space to take advantage of the late afternoon sun.

If they are an option, extra windows and skylights will let in
extra light. Inserting a skylight in a ceiling recess will create a
luminous lightwell and a dynamic architectural feature. To diffuse
or modulate light in excessively bright environments, or simply to
add a degree of separation between internal and external
worlds, screen windows or glass walls with muslin or wire mesh
panels. Alternatively, fit the ubiquitous roller blinds.

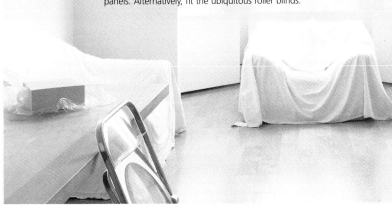

One of the big advantages of living in an open-plan space is the increased general access to and visual prominence of an original or new architectural feature of special interest. In a domestic space, this is often a key architectural feature that was formerly exclusive to one room, such as original ceiling mouldings, a decorative fireplace, or a large bay window. In an ex-industrial environment, original architectural features can act as fascinating reminders of a previous existence, and can also become an intrinsic part of a new scheme. For example, a pair of original steel loading-bay doors might inspire a utilitarian aesthetic, with rough, unfinished walls. Alternatively, a bold new architectural feature, such as a circular skylight, could become the central focus of a space.

ATURES ARE FASCINATING REMINDERS OF A VERY DIFFERENT PREVIOUS EXISTENCE

However, it's essential to consider the proportion and scale of the architectural features in a new open-plan environment. Some original features, such as a period fireplace, which have a powerful link to the previous interior arrangement, may look less impressive or out of place outside their original framework, consequently undermining the openness and unity of the new arrangement.

opposite above An adventurous conversion of a subterranean space maximizes the incoming light that floods in through a glass ceiling over one half of the space. As the brightest area, this is the obvious position for a relaxing zone and an internal garden.

above centre and right The distinctive barrel-vaulted ceiling was the starting point for this arrangement, with a large kitchen and dining zone occupying the centre of the interior and the bathing and sleeping areas arranged down one side of the space.

Change and review

For some people, open-plan living is a logical next step, representing a timely move away from conventional domestic interiors towards a more versatile, less formal living space. For others, it is a chance to explore a completely different way of living, one with a dynamic sense of freedom, space and light.

Before committing yourself to a complete change in lifestyle, think about your circumstances and the level of change you want. Take into account any potential changes in circumstance – if your family grows, where will the new arrivals be accommodated? Also look at different one-space options. There are many different ways to embrace the philosophy of open-plan living, and not all of them require a complete rejection of everything that is familiar and recognizable.

If open-plan living represents a radical move for you, possibly from a conventional house to a loft conversion, allow for a period of adjustment to this way of life before you undertake alterations. Everything is up for review, from how you organize and use your space to the levels of openness and sharing. Even existing furniture may require a rethink. Avoid snap decisions. Accept this as a challenge, one that requires imaginative design and planning solutions, but will ultimately lead to a more versatile and practical lifestyle.

opposite In a New York apartment, flexible curtain track and plastic sheeting separate off a sleeping area and diffuse the incoming light.

this page This expansive industrial conversion houses a series of separate yet interconnecting areas. Paper roller blinds make versatile dividers.

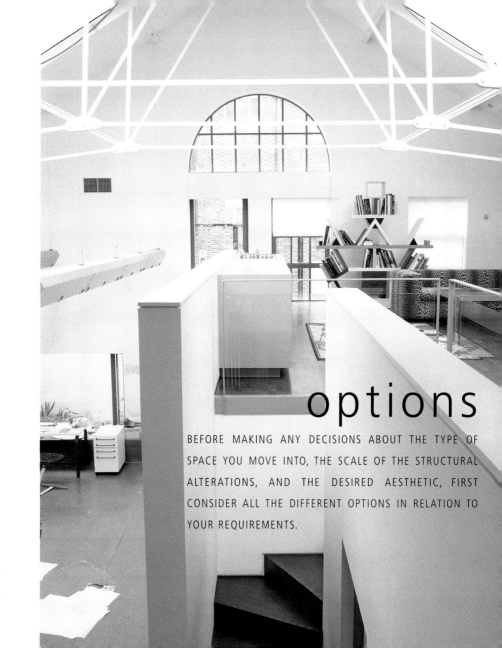

options

BEFORE MAKING ANY DECISIONS ABOUT THE TYPE OF SPACE YOU MOVE INTO, THE SCALE OF THE STRUCTURAL ALTERATIONS, AND THE DESIRED AESTHETIC, FIRST CONSIDER ALL THE DIFFERENT OPTIONS IN RELATION TO YOUR REQUIREMENTS.

Open-plan opportunities

There are essentially two different types of open-plan home – non-domestic spaces, such as ex-industrial units, or conventional properties, such as flats and houses, which are either original open-plan spaces or have been restructured into a single space.

Non-domestic space Ex-light industrial buildings often boast generous proportions and original details. They offer the opportunity to create a new and unique living environment. Although it is possible to develop such a building yourself, it is a huge job requiring frequent liaison with local council departments regarding planning permission, change of use (from non-domestic to domestic premises) and the supply of basic utilities. A venture of this kind is a huge undertaking. Finding a non-domestic building that can be converted to a single domestic unit is a different matter, one that is well worth the time and effort involved.

Perhaps the best option is a ready-made conversion. Look for those conversions that are sympathetic to the original building, and avoid those that disregard the building and have disappointingly conventional interiors as a result. It can be difficult to find units prior to development, but some developers allow or even invite input from future purchasers. If you see a building of interest undergoing conversion, make enquiries of the builders or developer and get in on the act of conversion as soon as possible. Once original details are lost, they are gone forever.

opposite A geometric division of a post-office sorting depot provides distinct activity areas for the artist owner's studio and living space.

above right and right Many non-domestic buildings offer diverse and fascinating options for conversion to open-plan homes.

left and opposite Removing the walls of an earlier conversion restored this space to its original proportions. The capsule kitchen is a tidy solution in a small space. **below left** A few minor yet effective adjustments brought this space up to date to provide a compact inner-city base.

Domestic space The benefit of domestic space is its wide availability and a familiar set of references. The interior dimensions, window sizes and ceiling heights are all relatively unchallenging. Such details can change with radical restructuring, but even the most inventive schemes cannot conceal the basic framework. And the basic framework of a domestic space is often an immediately recognizable one.

However, many domestic environments have great open-plan potential, and there are several options available, from individual houses to purpose-built apartments. Single or two storey buildings are a logical option. And while a house extending over three or four different levels is a more challenging option, it is not an unworkable one.

Many flats built since the 1950s already exhibit a degree of open-plan living, integrating day-to-day living activities as an expression of a new informality in contemporary lifestyles. Interestingly, a 1950s flat can impose a stricter sense of architectural correctness than an eighteenth-century house. The powerful aesthetics of 1950s, '60s and '70s architecture can dominate a scheme and inhibit a simple rationalization of the space.

As many period houses have been split into a series of smaller units, reverting a flat conversion to a single space often restores an interior's original dimensions and reinstates a sense of proportion and light. Windows regain their correct position and light can flow through an interior without the interruption of numerous partition walls.

opposite and far left
Transporting the side of a container truck into a former commercial space in New York introduces a powerful industrial aesthetic and divides the space into public and private areas. **left** The effect of using industrial elements like over-size ducting is decorative as well as functional.

New aesthetics

Choosing an aesthetic or interior style for your open-plan space – whether it is raw and industrial or a sleek design with high-spec finishes – will help you to direct every design and planning decision towards a consistent concept. Ideally, consider the aesthetics at the very beginning of a project. Knowing exactly how you want a space to look will provide a vital reference when you are choosing flooring and wall finishes, as well as deciding on how to divide space and what type of fixtures to install. In this way, the aesthetic is an integral part of a space, not a decorative add-on

An interior style that takes the original architecture of a building as the starting point for the scheme will bring visual definition to a space in a direct and unpretentious way. Conversely, imposing a random aesthetic that has no link to the architecture of a space, unless it is used to present a dynamic and consistent juxtaposition to the interior, will only detract and distract from any sense of unity. This is not a caution against introducing colour, comfort or possessions. All these elements can bring a strong new identity to a scheme. However, it is a caution against an assortment of discordant elements that do not fit together and will diminish an overall sense of space or visual simplicity.

With ex-industrial buildings, such as factories and workshops, a raw, hard-edged aesthetic is in keeping with the original architecture as well as any remaining structural details or industrial elements in the space. Retaining original features is a way of acknowledging the past existence of a space, too. Obliterating any sense of a building's

IDEALLY, YOU SHOULD CONSIDER THE AESTHETICS OF THE SPACE AT THE VERY BEGINNING OF A PROJECT, NOT AT THE END heritage or original purpose by overlayering every surface with a glossy new finish is a mistake. In a compact interior, where a sense of space is a key consideration, a minimal, pared-down aesthetic will streamline an interior and optimize space. If this style is to work, orderliness, tidiness and attention to detail are of paramount importance. Vigilance is everything. Edit your possessions and eliminate any redundant items. Clutter or excess furniture will only diminish a sense of space.

Stylistic contrasts between the architecture of a space and its contents can add a sense of excitement to a scheme by introducing a degree of friction. Exposed industrial or structural elements and modern upholstered furniture is an interesting combination. Keep to simple, sculptural shapes and a precise symmetrical arrangement of furniture.

Classical domestic architecture often suggests a traditional interior. However, reconfiguring such a space into an open-plan environment equipped with industrial fittings will enliven it with an unexpected element of contradiction. The juxtaposition will be particularly effective if you keep the structural elements and contents apart. Minimize the connections between the two by introducing freestanding fittings and furniture.

right The former sitting room of a large period townhouse was converted into a small open-plan apartment. To create a feeling of space and light, the interior has been stripped of all its traditional decorative features, leaving instead a pared-down, minimalist shell.

left Although this space is devoid of decorative objects, the overall design and mix of wood, marble, glass, steel and different planes of white create a visually stimulating yet orderly environment.

above In a voluminous New York loft, white ceilings and walls and a smooth concrete floor provide a low-key backdrop to a mix of furniture and artefacts with an Eastern influence.

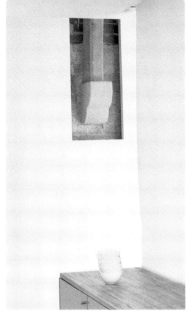

Structural change

Imaginative planning and design can bring about dramatic spatial transformations and result in the best possible use of the available space and light in an interior. Less radical yet equally inspirational schemes can reorganize space in a way that will provide an efficient framework for living that suits current requirements, while still retaining a degree of flexibility to accommodate future change.

opposite, above and above right This bold conversion of a former schoolhouse sensitively juxtaposes new and original features to create a bold and dynamic contemporary environment. The lower floor is a spacious living area with staircases leading to mezzanine levels at each end.

With any level of structural change, it is essential to be aware of planning restrictions and to follow any regulations. This is particularly the case with units in a block, historic houses and buildings of special architectural interest, or if you want to make changes to the exterior of a building. If you remove a structural or load-bearing wall, it is necessary to add a concrete, metal or timber beam to support the opening. The size of the beam depends on how much weight it must support. Knocking through new openings, adding mezzanine levels, or removing part of the floor may all require additional support. Some non-domestic buildings can tolerate alterations without additional strengthening. However, it is essential to check with relevant planning departments, a surveyor or a structural engineer before undertaking structural alterations. And even the simplest structural changes may also require changes to the utilities and service systems. They may also be subject to regulations, so seek professional advice about any alterations.

Assessment and action

Whether you are contemplating low-level alterations or radical change, assessing your requirements is the first step.

The main issues to consider are how best to use the available space, how to integrate several different activity zones and how to give visual definition to the whole interior. Whether you live as a couple or a family, taking into account everyone's requirements is a complex process. Yet it will provide you with essential information and indicate any areas that are in need of change or improvement. It will also focus time, effort and creativity on finding workable, economical solutions.

Begin by listing all the different ways in which you use your space. Run through the events of a typical weekday and weekend and list every activity that takes place in your home. Which activities are public or social? Which activities require privacy or isolation? Do conflicts of interest arise as a result of different activities? If you have young children, make two lists for every child, one that covers the child's current requirements, and one that covers the child's requirements five years from now. All this information will indicate ways in which you can organize and combine activities, with different degrees of privacy and openness. It will also provide an essential checklist for any planning or design decisions. Make use of it to keep changes and developments moving in the right direction, in line with your expectations.

opposite left Floor-to-ceiling paper blinds screen off a work area tucked away in a corner and separate it from the main body of the space.

opposite right If cooking and eating are key activities in your home, position the kitchen at the centre of your space. This kitchen's vibrant colour signals its important role.

this page This sleeping area strikes a comfortable balance between connection with the living area and a sense of privacy.

BEFORE YOU MAKE ANY FINAL DECISIONS, TAKE TIME TO INVESTIGATE EVERY OPTION

Now that you know exactly what you need from your space, assess it as it currently exists. Include any positive or negative observations. Look objectively at the volume and dimensions. Draw a rough floorplan and note the general layout and the position of the facilities and utilities. Map out the circulation routes around the space and note any areas of congestion or inconvenient restrictions. Chart the way that light enters and moves around the space, indicating the different areas it animates at different times of day.

Finally, you can review all the information about your current and future requirements together with your observations about the space. Before you make any final decisions, take time to ponder on all the possible improvements, to discuss and review your ideas in depth and to investigate every option.

Now is the time to set your budget, investigate any restrictions to possible changes and decide on acceptable levels of disruption and time limits. If you are contemplating large-scale structural changes, a major reorganization of space, or changes to the existing utilities, this is the moment to bring in the professionals for expert advice and creative input.

The end result of analysing every aspect of a project in this way is a clear objective and a precise step-by-step plan of action. Regardless of the level of change you are planning, your aim is to find the most practical and economical way ahead. Employing builders, beginning work and then changing tack will increase costs considerably. If at all possible, avoid making any changes to your plans once work has commenced and is underway. It will save you money and prevent any potential delays as well as helping you to maintain a good working relationship with your builders!

left A light-industrial space is given an inexpensive makeover with white paint and structural add-ons, including a diagonal division between living and working areas and a step up to a sleeping zone. The result is a simple, comfortable space with a welcoming sense of space, openness and light.

help

FOR COMPLEX PROJECTS OR ALTERATIONS THAT AFFECT THE
BASIC STRUCTURE OF THE SERVICES IN A PROPERTY, SOME
FORM OF SPECIALIST GUIDANCE IS ESSENTIAL.

Architects, surveyors, engineers and builders

Most projects break down into three stages: planning and design, administration and supervision (checking building regulations and applying for planning permissions), and the actual building work. For extensive and complex projects, it is important to employ professionals to design, plan and manage the work. For less complex alterations, it is possible to involve experts in only certain aspects of the job – to employ an architect to design and plan the project without overseeing the work, for example.

opposite and above In a conventional domestic interior it is not always possible to remove walls or radically reconfigure space. Simple devices like inserting internal windows and widening existing openings can transform a space and introduce a new sense of connection.

Architects An architect brings vision and experience to a project, guaranteeing the best possible result in terms of creativity and cost-efficiency. As well as planning and design, an architect can suggest materials, find specialist contractors or manufacturers to provide fixtures and fittings, and recommend a good builder. The basis of a good working relationship is trust, communication and confidence, so meet and talk to architects whose work you like, or ask friends for recommendations. Ask to see photos of recent projects, or visit them yourself.

Chartered surveyors Chartered surveyors offer advice on all aspects of buying and selling property. If you are contemplating buying a property or making structural changes to your current property, a survey will provide essential information about the condition of the building. It will point out any defects, which may influence your decision to buy, or indicate areas that are in need of improvement and development.

Structural engineers Structural engineers will assess a building's structure and stability. Areas for consideration include the foundations, walls, columns, beams and roof components. A structural engineer can specify materials, prepare technical drawings, check regulations and restrictions and obtain relevant consents and permissions, prepare costings and monitor the actual building work.

Builders The best option for finding a builder is personal recommendation. If you are employing an architect or a structural engineer, they may be able to suggest builders to undertake your project. Alternatively, trade associations can recommend local builders. Be precise about your requirements – prepare a detailed written brief and ask the builder for a written estimate.

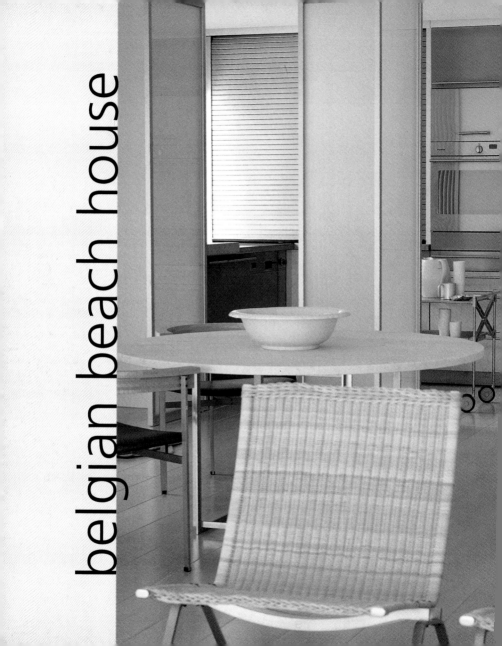

belgian beach house

SPACIOUS SEASIDE APARTMENT

This radical transformation of a contemporary yet conventional weekend home in a coastal town in Belgium allows the owners maximum flexibility. The new open-plan scheme significantly improves the use of space, the light distribution and access to sea views. Now a translucent environment with a sense of spaciousness that is entirely in keeping with its location, the apartment offers a refreshing escape from urban life.

In an ideal location overlooking the sea, this apartment is a long rectangular space that runs the full length of an uninspiring purpose-built block, with expansive windows and outdoor terraces at either end. Standard windows ranged down one side of the space look out on to an identical building next door. The original interior – an unimaginative domestic layout with poor light distribution and restricted sea views – did not optimize the positive assets of the space.

The architects' new scheme comprises large open areas at both ends of the apartment, which make excellent use of the wonderful light and views. At the front of the apartment, a spacious living, dining and kitchen area overlooks the sea, while at the back, the tranquil sleeping area faces inwards towards the town. A sequence of individual work, storage, shower and bathing areas are lined up in between, connecting the two ends of the apartment.

Large moving panels of opaque glass and wood provide multiple possibilities for opening or enclosing every area and subdividing the space as a whole.

floor plan This modern apartment consists of a long, thin rectangular space with large windows at either end and all along one outside wall. Versatile sliding panels divide the front and back of the apartment into two zones, public and private, with additional smaller subdivisions for working, bathing and storage areas neatly sandwiched in between.

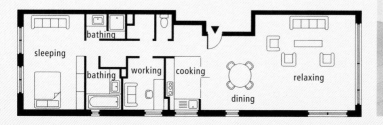

sleeping

bathing

bathing

working

cooking

dining

relaxing

opposite inset above and centre The kitchen area is a series of flexible divisions, from the stainless steel shutters that screen the work surface to the movable glass panels that enclose it.

this page A corridor running the length of the apartment links the sleeping and living areas. Wood or glass panels slide across the corridor to create a sense of separation.

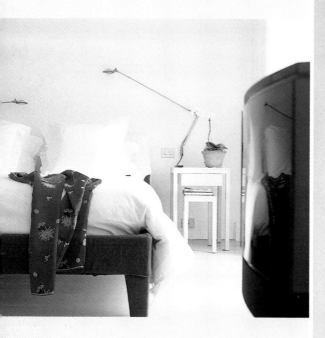

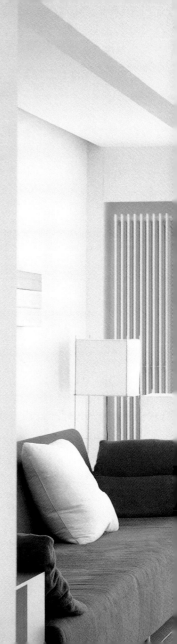

A wooden panel that slides across the corridor divides the apartment into two sections, while a glass panel in a similar position offers a very different degree of separation. The moving panels underline and facilitate the architects' intention to provide flexible, optional divisions between a front-of-house area and the back-of-house facilities. And while the new organization of space retains an element of the original layout, with the sitting and kitchen areas on the sea side of the apartment and sleeping and bathing on the town side, the experience of being in the space is radically different.

Surrounding the kitchen area with glass panels continues the principle of flexibility. When closed, the panels create an opaque box, rather like an abstract art installation. As the panels open or slide across, the area reconfigures, and the sightlines from and access to the kitchen change. Four independent panels facing the sea pivot inwards or outwards in multiple variations,

opposite left The sleeping area is a secondary relaxing zone, with inviting furniture, a television and several different lighting options.
far left The sitting room is tranquil and inviting, complete with natural light, soft seating and a low table for drinks or books.
left A desk fitted into a narrow alcove provides a useful work space.

reflecting and refracting light with their every movement. Each glass panel projects monochromatic images and shadows, enlivening the space with a new landscape and extra dimensions.

Other reflective surfaces throughout the space catch and throw back light and shadows with similar effect. The sycamore flooring running from front to back (except in the shower and bathing areas), the stainless steel kitchen worktops, equipment and shuttering and the expansive mirrors all contribute to an effect of luminosity and a special quality of light.

White roller blinds at every window moderate the incoming light, reduce glare and maintain a temperate environment. Changing the position of the blinds also alters the focus of the space. With the blinds down, the light is diffused and a sense of enclosure is created. When the blinds are up, revealing views of the ever-changing sea and sky, there is a sense of exposure to the elements and connection with the world outside.

zoning

relaxing I cooking I bathing I sleeping I working

ORGANIZING AN OPEN-PLAN ENVIRONMENT IS ABOUT COMBINING DIFFERENT ACTIVITIES INTO A LOGICAL SEQUENCE OF INTERCONNECTING ZONES. DESIGNATING A WELL-LIT, OPEN AREA AS A RELAXING ZONE WILL PROVIDE A WELCOMING ENVIRONMENT, SOMEWHERE TO BE AT EASE WITH FAMILY AND FRIENDS.

relaxing

An open-plan interior incorporates many different activities, and dividing these activities into zones facilitates good organization and the optimum use of space. Few zones are dedicated to a single activity – the majority combine several related activities, such as cooking and eating, or reading and listening to music. Unlike a conventional domestic environment, which has set divisions between different zones, an open-plan environment is about flexibility and integration. So the way a zone relates to the general space is just as important as the way it functions in its own right.

There's no set formula for organizing zones within a space – everyone has different requirements and every space will suggest a different solution. Obviously, it makes sense to take advantage of well-lit areas for relaxing, eating and cooking zones, but the amount of space devoted to each activity is a matter of individual preference. It's important to assess your personal requirements and structure the main

opposite In a light, open workshop conversion, a high-level storage panel in the kitchen area separates front-of-house and back-of-house activities.

left A sliding panel is an ingenious flexible storage solution for a multi-functional relaxing zone, and brings vibrant colour to a light, white space.

living area to suit your lifestyle. If you enjoy social activities such as entertaining, this suggests one way to organize your space. If you enjoy more solitary pursuits, such as listening to music, this suggests a different arrangement.

In a multi-functional relaxing zone, where many activities coexist and overlap, a flexible arrangement of furniture, storage and lighting is essential. The style and position of furniture and the lighting effects will define and facilitate everyday use and enjoyment of the zone.

When choosing furniture, consider the scale and architecture of your interior. In an expansive loft, for example, a geometric arrangement of big sofas and

a central low table will anchor a relaxing zone. Soft textures and shapes can provide an interesting juxtaposition with industrial concrete flooring or other non-domestic details. In smaller spaces, beware of allowing oversized pieces to dominate the space, as they may compromise the overall flexibility and versatility of the zone.

A configuration of chairs is often the main indicator of a relaxing zone, establishing a general style and indicating the level of informality. Different chairs fit different activities, so aim to provide a selection of soft (easy) and hard (upright) seating to meet your requirements and to define different activities. For example,

group armchairs together for general conversation, position a recliner on its own for quiet reading, and gather upright chairs together around a table for eating. Sofas often end up as a big seat for one person, so don't feel you should automatically include one. If you enjoy putting your feet up, a chaise longue or daybed may be a better option, as they take up less space and are often more comfortable. On a practical note, single chairs are easier to move and reconfigure into different seating arrangements and therefore are more versatile.

A selection of stools and storage cubes offer space-efficient supplementary seating – ideal for the occasional influx of people – and also function as side tables

this page In a typical multi-functional living space, arrangements of furniture and lighting suggest different activities. A classic sofa, low table and task lighting provide a comfortable place for reading and relaxing.

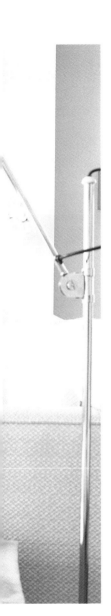

opposite far left In an open-plan apartment, a table and chairs in a quiet setting by a window provide an alternative to the main dining table.
above A narrow lobby off the main living space is furnished with easy chairs and a rug to provide an informal seating area.

for the phone, a pile of books or a coffee cup. Floor cushions add an informal note, as well as providing child-friendly seating options. A bed is an inexpensive alternative to chairs. It can provide a comfortable communal seating area and works well in either a big space or a small studio. Choose a bed base on wheels for maximum flexibility, and throw on a cover to protect and conceal pillows and duvets. Store bed linen elsewhere or, if the bed is high enough, in boxes beneath it. Some divans come with built-in storage space in the base.

Accessible and flexible storage solutions will help create a sense of organization and maintain a sense of space. Books, television sets, CD players, CDs, DVD players, DVDs, board and computer games all require shelf space. Finding a place for everything is a challenge, but designing and putting together

below left A mobile trolley allows a television to be wheeled out for viewing then stored out of sight when not in use.
below right Somewhere to sit away from the main living area, like these chairs and table grouped on a mezzanine level, offers an alternative setting for peaceful relaxation.

efficient storage will go a long way towards preventing chaos. However, if everything is hidden from view an area can look austere. Strike a balance – display favourite items and store the rest out of sight.

Mobile trolleys are a big bonus in an open-plan environment, enabling you to move heavy pieces of entertainment equipment around easily and relocate them when they are not in use. For example, you can push a large-screen television into a central area for viewing then wheel it out of sight afterwards.

Some storage solutions take advantage of the structure of a space to provide inventive options. Fitting a bookcase into a narrow recess makes use of an otherwise empty space and provides unobtrusive storage. Make the

most of alcoves or recesses by using them to house storage units or display space.

Creative lighting is an important factor in a relaxing zone. Different combinations of lights signal different moods, from bright and upbeat to low-key and intimate. Subtle ambient lighting is ideal for relaxing and entertaining and a central fitting on a dimmer switch can deliver this effect. Accent lighting enlivens an environment by introducing contrasting areas of light and shade, while task lighting directs a pool of light to illuminate a specific activity. Lighting design is a complex issue. If you plan to install a new lighting system, consult an expert. However, investing in floor lights to supplement a central fitting and wall lights will provide scope for many different combinations.

this page An expansive double-height window in a New York loft is a compelling backdrop to a comfortable seating area.

london purpose-built

MODERN CITY APARTMENT

This compact apartment is only a few minutes' walk from the owner's design studio. A strong architectural aesthetic combined with the convenience of a buzzing inner-city location makes this small space an inspiring base. Ingenious alterations have successfully updated the space by acknowledging the spirit of the original concept without creating a set piece of design history.

This small apartment, one of a series of open-plan single or double occupancy units, is situated on the top floor of a low-rise block in an inner-city location. The block is part of a 1950s council-housing complex originally built for local blue-collar professionals such as nurses and the police.

With a Grade II listing to protect the existing space and limit any changes, acknowledging and understanding the history of the apartment is an important part of the owner/occupier package and adds to the excitement of living here – even though regulations and restrictions can sometimes protect the wrong thing, like an unauthentic replacement kitchen. So while the owner's ambition is restoration, even returning the kitchen to something like its original simplicity now requires planning permission.

The apartment's full-width arched window and barrel-shaped ceiling are exclusive to the top-floor units in the block and contribute to the high levels of light and general sense of space. The wall

of glass outlines a panoramic view over east London. This view, and the overall impression of luminosity and space, are the first things that strike you upon entering the apartment, drawing the eye straight past the kitchen area, which is set to one side of the entrance, and into the main living area beyond.

Seventy per cent of the space is occupied by a living area that contains different seating configurations that define different activities. There are chairs arranged around a table for eating or

this page and opposite The view from the entrance shows the kitchen area at the left, sitting area directly ahead, and the sleeping area to the right.

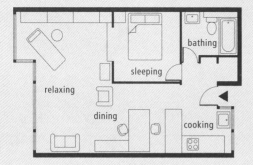

floor plan The apartment is a compact rectangle, with a glass wall in front of the relaxing zone. Attention to detail on the part of the original architects means that there are several storage solutions built into the kichen and relaxing areas – vital in a space of this size.

working, chairs positioned for contemplating the view from the window, and a group configuration with a sofa for conversation and socializing. A solitary lounger, reading light and occasional table together with a large collection of design and photographic books signal the key area of interest and activity. The simple storage system for books is one of the new additions to the space. Running the full length of the living area, the shelving provides an ingenious opportunity for both storage and display.

In full view from the lounger, the sleeping zone is an open box set one step up from the main living area. The change in level, the wall panel intersecting the storage unit and the chain curtain are all new additions. The wall and the chain divider provide an ingenious division between areas without compromising the ease of transition or challenging the sense of overall openness. They underline what is remarkable about this compact space. Different areas interconnect in a logical sequence, yet also manage to convey a sense of independence and change in style specific to their different functions.

left Hanging a simple chain-link curtain across the opening between the main sitting area and the sleeping zone provides an inventive but effective screen that provides some privacy but retains a sense of openness.

above left An inexpensive shelving tower provides storage for shirts and other clothing. Castors have been attached to the base, so it can be spun round to face the wall, leaving a single neat shelf on view.

WITH RESOURCEFUL PLANNING, IT IS POSSIBLE TO
DESIGN A HIGH-PERFORMANCE, USER-FRIENDLY
KITCHEN AREA. CLEVER DIVIDERS AND WELL-
THOUGHT-OUT STORAGE WILL ADD FLEXIBILITY
AND VERSATILITY AND FACILITATE INTEGRATION
WITH THE REST OF YOUR SPACE.

cooking

When planning and designing a kitchen area, think about its frequency of use, ease of access and its position in your interior. Look at the relationship between cooking and eating. Do you cook every day or do you simply use the kitchen to heat up ready-made meals? How many people does the kitchen cater for? The size and prominence of a kitchen area should reflect its role in your day-to-day life. So be realistic in your evaluation – getting it wrong and overstating or underplaying a kitchen area is a waste of an opportunity, effort, and space.

Before you decide to rearrange your space to accommodate a new kitchen area or change around an existing installation, check the utilities and services. Water supplies and drainage are essential services that require access to external walls. It may be

above left and centre Precision fixtures and fittings, like these high-specification stainless steel units, utensils and worktops, create a minimalist look.
above A capsule kitchen hides behind retractable doors.
opposite In a city apartment used for weekend breaks, the compact kitchen-in-a-cupboard is exactly the right size for use.

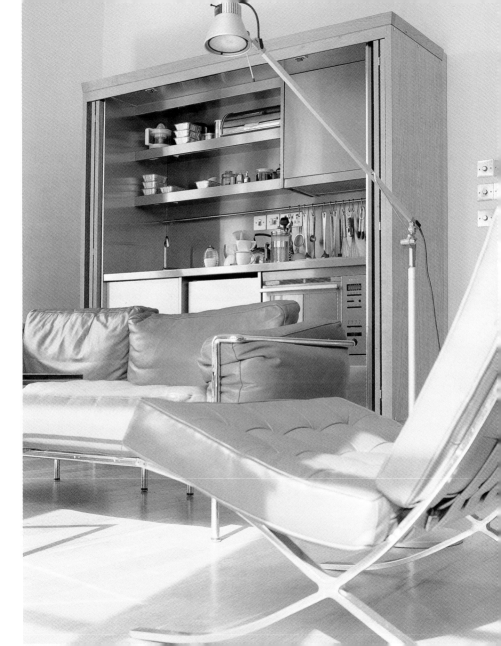

above top and bottom
Clever ideas like fitting
an oven in the end of a
table and slotting in a
fridge beneath steps to
a mezzanine level
maximize space in a
compact and minimalist
kitchen area.

above Long wooden
benches, which can be
neatly tucked away
beneath the table when
not in use, are a space-
saving seating solution
that is ideally suited to
this simple and clutter-
free cooking zone.

opposite Integrating a
high-specification food
preparation area,
complete with two-ring
hob and circular kitchen
sink, with a dining
table, is an ingenious
use of the available
space in a kitchen.

possible to update or extend existing systems to allow a change in position of a kitchen area, although if a system is deficient or out of date, a complete refit is the best option. Drainage and waste pipes require a minimum gradient, so position sinks, dishwashers and washing machines within reasonable distance of an external outlet. Plan new piping with as few twists and bends as possible, to reduce the risk of blockages.

Good ventilation removes excess moisture from the atmosphere and prevents cooking smells from invading the rest of the space (this is a sensible precaution if, for example, clothes are kept in an open storage system). Open windows go a long way to keep fresh air circulating, yet high-specification cooking equipment can produce excessive amounts of moisture that will eventually damage the fabric of an environment. And while smell is a powerful and vital stimulant in the preparation, cooking and eating process, the lingering smell of yesterday's food is not quite as appealing. However, a quick session with an extractor fan will soon clear the air. For direct effect, install an extractor unit above cooking equipment or, to provide good general ventilation, fit extractor fans in walls and windows.

Orientation is an important factor within the kitchen area itself and affects its integration with the overall space. For example, fitting a low-level line of units along an outside wall, possibly with a

window with a pleasant view, focuses a
kitchen area, and anyone working in it,
away from the rest of the space. Standing
at the work-surface preparing food or
cooking will involve turning your back on
everything else. If you like to work away
from any distraction, possibly in isolation,
then this is a good option.

Fitting an identical arrangement of
low-level units away from the wall, with
access from both sides so people can
walk around the unit, will transform the
orientation of your kitchen area and the
experience of being in it. If you live with
young children who require your
attention, or like cooking to be a social
event, this is a practical arrangement.
Likewise, dividing a kitchen into two
parallel lines of units, or locating
everything in a central unit or block, will
involve different movements around the
kitchen area and create different
connections with the overall space.

this picture Parallel
high- and low-level
cabinets accommodate
an efficient kitchen
with easy access to the
ample storage space.

opposite Providing a place to sit, like these stools attached to the end of a worktop, signal the kitchen area as a social place.
below Power sockets set flush in a worktop facilitate efficiency and convenience and avoid the hazard of trailing power leads.

below Two sliding panels at the end of this functional galley kitchen area provide varying degrees of separation from the rest of the space and modulate the flow of light.

opposite above In a converted former schoolhouse, the compact kitchen area is slotted in beneath a mezzanine level and overlooks a double-height eating and relaxing zone.

opposite below Flat panels flip down to conceal the work-surfaces and the food preparation area, while a roller blind between the kitchen and eating areas screens mess.

If your kitchen area is also intended to be a social place, take this into account in the planning and design. Include broad work-surfaces with access from both sides, and put stools around a work-surface to encourage people to participate or spectate. However, it's important to pay attention to safety issues. Do not invite people to sit next to a hazardous hot surface. Keep seating away from the main work triangle between cooking unit, sink and work-surface. And for general efficiency and safety, incorporate heat-proof surfaces alongside cooking units, so the cook can avoid walking around with hot pots and pans. Ideally, provide somewhere comfortable where guests or family can sit close by, but away from the general work traffic. A sense of openness, easy access and light will promote the kitchen area as a friendly, welcoming environment.

Apart from installing a cooking unit and plumbing in a kitchen sink, there is no reason to permanently fix anything else in one place. Mobile work-surfaces, kitchen tables and storage units will all add versatility to a kitchen area and make your working environment responsive to your changing requirements. Even in a compact kitchen area, including a single mobile unit and storing it out of the way under a work-surface or in a built-in cupboard will increase overall flexibility.

Creating a kitchen with different, varying levels of enclosure and openness increases flexibility and versatility. Simple ideas like a pull-down shutter or sliding screen to enclose a cooking unit can shift the focus of a kitchen area away from the function of preparing large family meals to simple low-key activities like making a single cup of coffee. This change in emphasis and appearance introduces new possibilities for use, changing the dynamic from that of a hard-working area to a more low-key and informal one. Alternatively, it's possible to use lighting to transfer emphasis from one activity area to another.

Streamlining the industrial elements of a kitchen area into a single panel or unit can add efficiency and visual simplicity to an arrangement. Planning a kitchen area as a series of logical and ergonomic workstations, perhaps with one low-level and one high-level unit, will optimize the available space. One solution to

left and below In a remarkably compact kitchen area, a glass panel fixed over the stairwell is a clever idea that allows light to reach the staircase and also creates another worksurface. Open shelves provide extra storage space.

a small space is to integrate cooking and eating areas into a single central workbench, with an oven and hob built in at one end and a separate storage unit elsewhere. This approach does not preclude display and open storage, which can add vitality and individuality to an area, but it is a caution against overcrowding or clutter.

Keep an open mind about the layout and aesthetics of a kitchen until you have finalized the location and structure. While thinking about how you will organize the area is a critical part of the decision-making process, setting your heart on an industrial aesthetic, for example, with stainless steel equipment and work-surfaces, may not be the best solution for integrating the area into the rest of your space. Sometimes the best option is a compromise of aesthetics, cost-efficiency and practicality. An efficient scheme that makes good use of space is far preferable to an unworkable or over-complex arrangement of set pieces.

Choose fittings and equipment that are compatible with the scale and general style of the interior. Standard fixtures and fittings can look out of scale in a loft space – this type of environment offers an opportunity to use bold architectural statements and unconventional elements, such as concrete work-surfaces and industrial-style lighting. In a compact interior, choose sleek precision elements to maximize the available space. Slim dishwashers and washing machines offer useful alternatives to standard-width equipment and can make all the difference between an efficient area and a labour-intensive one.

london industrial unit

Converting a raw industrial unit to domestic use is an exciting
opportunity to devise an entirely original and individual place to live.
Taking on a project of this size and complexity, co-ordinating and
designing every aspect personally without any previous experience, and
producing such an uncompromisingly modern scheme, as the owner of
this space did, is a triumph of vision and determination.

top left and above left Many of the kitchen fittings are ex-industrial. The anglepoise lamps are old hospital fixtures and bring a stark aesthetic to the food-preparation area.

top right and above right Everyday items such as bowls, utensils, pots and pans are kept close at hand on old catering trolleys. **right** A section of the upper floor was cut out to provide access and light to the lower level of the apartment, making it possible to stand in the living area and peer over the banisters into the kitchen area below.

This exceptional apartment was once part of a printing works in London's East End. The owner bought an empty space on two levels with no existing connections, just rough concrete floors, bare brick walls, large windows on the upper level, inadequate light on the lower level and no basic utilities. Now, after conversion, this industrial unit is now a unique home and work space for the owner, a food writer and art director, and his partner. Given the professional food angle, the style and position of the kitchen is a big factor in the scheme of things.

Initial plans sited the kitchen area on the upper level, at the end of the main living space alongside the original loading-bay doors, to allow street-level access after food shopping. However, the owner decided against installing a kitchen in full view of the main living area, where it would be the visual focus of the space, instead allocating it a key position of power and significance on the lower level. After a radical spatial reworking, including the removal of part of the floor on the upper level and the insertion of a glass walkway and connecting stairway to the lower level, the kitchen is the new centre of the space, with all other areas radiating outwards from this magnetic core.

The kitchen area embodies the industrial aesthetic running throughout the apartments. It is all steel and concrete, with a battery of expensive professional catering equipment built in alongside more eclectic freestanding second-hand finds and salvaged pieces. Despite the absence of colour, except during food preparation, it is still a vibrant and visually stimulating area. When viewed from the gallery in the main living area above, the kitchen looks welcoming yet low-key.

An external door at the top of a flight of stairs from the basement, one of four separate entrances to the unit, provides access after food shopping trips. Other hidden assets tucked away behind the kitchen area include structural alcoves and cave-like storage spaces that provide a generous pantry and scullery. Small-scale areas like these offset the expansiveness of the general space and add an essential element of intimacy.

The sleeping area is screened from the kitchen by a glass dividing wall and sliding clear glass panel. And beyond the

sleeping area, behind a wooden panel, are a bath and shower. Here again, witty juxtapositions add vitality to the scheme. High-specification fixtures and fittings like underfloor heating and wall-to-wall mosaic tiling co-exist with salvaged bath taps and radiators and project an air of relaxed urban sophistication.

Up the open steel and plywood stairs and via a glass walkway lit from below is the main living area. The horizontal lines of the long, low, pale sofas and fireplace emphasize the unusual height and scale of the area. A length of tracing paper hanging from a thin metal rod in front of the original loading-bay doors conceals an original yet unpopular architectural feature. The paper diffuses light, reduces the view of a development site opposite and screens the interior from passers-by.

Except for the mosaic tiles in the bath and shower area, the flooring throughout the space is concrete paving slabs. Three applications of sealant were applied to protect the highly absorbent surface. High-spec underfloor heating takes the chill off this modest element – yet another juxtaposition of exclusive and low-budget elements in this dramatic and unpretentious conversion.

right The plump outlines of second-hand sofas offset the new, more elemental concrete floors and walls, and present a new interpretation of the traditional lounge area.

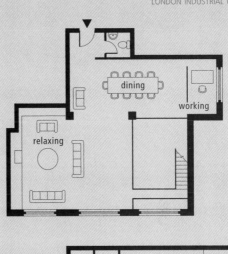

floor plan The apartment is situated on two levels, with part of the upper level cut away to allow light and access to the basement level. Cast concrete steps with plywood treads connect the two different levels and lead, via a glass walkway, from the tranquil sitting area down into the kitchen zone

opposite above left In keeping with the industrial aesthetic, a sheet of mirror leans up against the back of the iroko wood divider between the bathing and sleeping areas.

opposite above right Unlike standard bathroom fittings, the scale and functional designs of hospital or laboratory taps fit perfectly with the dimensions of an industrial conversion.

opposite below left and right The monumental panel of iroko wood that divides the sleeping and bathing areas is also a headboard for the bed. The deep tones of the wood provides a dramatic contrast to the blue mosaic tiles that line the bathing zone beyond.

right The bathing area incorporates a number of salvaged fixtures and fittings, yet the light and space, and warmth from underfloor heating pipes, create an underlying sense of luxury.

below Sliding panels of textured glass divide an informal family bathing zone from a sleeping area. **below right** A solid panel that is housed in a recess in the wall can be swung across the corridor to divide the public and private areas of a loft apartment. **opposite** A bold combination of strong colours, textures and shapes enlivens this spacious communal bathing area in a New York loft.

COMMUNAL OR SEPARATE, COLOURFUL OR LOW-KEY, HIGH-TECH OR FUNCTIONAL – PLANNING A SUCCESSFUL BATHING AREA IS ALL ABOUT FINDING A SOLUTION THAT OPTIMIZES THE AVAILABLE SPACE AND FITS IN WITH YOUR LIFESTYLE.

bathing

A bathing area is a place where you are naked and accordingly at your most vulnerable. Consider how you feel about this in terms of providing an open or communal bathing area – it is likely that some degree of enclosure and separation is an essential practical concession. If communal bathing and showering is acceptable to you and your family, yet the lavatory is one area requiring enclosure, then design and plan your bathing zone accordingly, or provide a separate lavatory in a different location. Direct access to a lavatory is preferable to walking past the bath or through a shower room.

opposite A sculptural, curving wall screens a tiny bathing zone. Access to the shower is by the window, while at the opposite end of the wall is the door to a separate lavatory. **above** A wall of waterproof plaster curls around the tiny shower area and screens it from the main sleeping area without separating the two zones.

If you share a bathing zone, especially with young children, consider the many different requirements and schedules that will govern its use. In a family, the mornings are often rush hour. Everyone is showering or cleaning teeth together or in quick succession. Providing an extra shower room will reduce congestion. Even if you live alone, there will be times when guests are staying and competing with you for the facilities. A separate lavatory is useful if your bathing and sleeping zones are integrated, as it provides a place for visitors to use and directs general traffic away from a potentially private area.

It is logical to integrate sleeping and bathing zones in some way and provide a sense of division or separation from the rest of your space. It's possible to divide an interior into a public front-of-house space, containing the relaxing, cooking and eating zones, and a private back-of-house space that holds the sleeping and bathing zones. The layout of your space may naturally suggest a degree of separation – perhaps locating sleeping and bathing zones on a mezzanine level, or at one end of the property. A sliding or moving panel can reinforce this sense of division as well as providing privacy, reducing noise and maintaining a comfortable and constant temperature.

Creating a solid division between public and private zones, possibly a wood or plasterboard sliding or fixed panel, demarcates space effectively. A division of this kind provides an opportunity for greater freedom and openness in planning and designing sleeping and bathing zones. For a family, this option also presents an opportunity to have a more informal private zone layout with communal relaxation and play areas.

Glass screens and sliding doors fit well with the functional aspect of bathing zones. Opaque or textured glass makes an ideal divider between sleeping and bathing areas and offers the advantage of privacy and enclosure without the disadvantage of blocking light. Be warned that opaque glass is less opaque when wet, so condensation and shower spray will affect its transparency. Also, it is less effective as a screen if it is in close proximity to whatever it is screening. However, for wonderful light diffusion and pure luminosity it is worth making a few

exceptions. Fabric dividers like muslin or voile provide an inexpensive and atmospheric enclosure for a bath and define a place for relaxation. Warmth and low-key lighting will aid this essential process. Position a bath beside a window for a view of trees and sky. Or use candles to counterbalance a functional aesthetic and change the dynamic of a space. Install a dimmer control on artificial lights and use low-level lighting to signal a change in pace and aid relaxation.

Take into account the structure and dimensions of a bathing zone and its overall aesthetic when choosing fittings. For example, a space-saving minuscule shower and basin capsule requires high-specification compact fixtures and fittings that are in line with the general streamlined effect. Simple and precise elements like mixer taps, a built-in storage unit and a rigid shower-head work well in this type of environment.

above A wall of folding panels open and close to reveal and conceal a capsule bathing area with a shower enclosure slotted beyond.

left and far left High specification fixtures and fittings optimize space in the compact shower enclosure. Horizontal bars set over a vertically hung radiator create a practical towel rail.

opposite above Make the most of high ceilings by creating platforms or mezzanine levels. Here, a sleeping platform is stacked atop a bathing area.

opposite below Tucked in beneath the sleeping platform, this small bathroom has no direct source of light, so relies on a glazed internal window to increase light levels.

At the opposite end of the scale, a conversion of a former industrial space with raw brickwork and surface piping requires bold and generous fixtures and fittings that are in keeping with the utilitarian aesthetic. A concrete bath with mosaic tiling and a huge salvaged shower-head that projects water on to a sloping floor are appropriate choices, in proportion with the original industrial fittings throughout the space.

Unconventional fixtures and fittings can provide unpretentious and inexpensive alternatives to standard products. Laboratory taps, basins and medicine cabinets create a strong effect and guarantee reliable, long-term performance. Shop display or hotel fittings, such as combination hooks for clothing, extending rails and metal shelving, offer hard-working storage for accessories and towels. Commercial kitchen suppliers offer lots of inspiration and inexpensive products. Stainless steel sinks, ceramic hand-basins for professional kitchens, and metal and plastic storage bins all transfer easily into a domestic bathing zone.

If you plan to use standard fixtures, opt for simple shapes in white. Introduce colour, texture, or contrast with flooring, tiles, or paint. A one-off item like a Japanese-style cedar bath, wooden basin or a simple bamboo mat adds organic warmth and texture. Contrasts between textures and materials, such as wood and ceramic, or concrete and glass, will enliven a potentially uniform area.

Architectural devices, like a curving dividing wall between a bathing and sleeping zone, a round shower enclosure or an opaque glass screen, will offset clinical hard edges with sculptural forms and shadows. Simple yet inventive details like these add individuality and, if visible from outside, present a new perspective to the overall space.

SLEEP IS A VITAL AND RESTORATIVE ACTIVITY. WHETHER YOU DEDICATE A PROMINENT AREA TO YOUR SLEEPING ZONE, OR SIMPLY INSTALL A FOLD-UP BED, PROVIDING A COMFORTABLE AND RESTFUL SLEEPING ENVIRONMENT IS ESSENTIAL FOR INDIVIDUAL WELL-BEING.

sleeping

left In an expansive New York loft, oriental screens and muslin drapes divide a sleeping area from the main space and provide texture and contrast to the raw industrial infrastructure.
right A muslin tent transforms a simple pine bed into an intimate retreat and adds a final layer of separation within a sleep zone.

Light is a big factor when allocating an area for sleep. Depending on your personal preference, waking up to bright morning light is either an invigorating experience or an unwelcome one. If access to direct light is important to you, then position a sleeping area by a window or beneath a skylight. If morning light is not a priority, then save the good light option for another zone, perhaps cooking or relaxing.

Dedicating a zone to sleeping is a wonderful opportunity to create a retreat from the outside world and provide ideal conditions for rest. If you share your life with a partner, children or friends, time alone is a precious event. A sleeping zone that offers a degree of separation can offer the perfect haven for a restorative or contemplative episode at any time of day.

Building a high bed base can add to a general sense of separation, while a lightweight fabric tent draped around a bed will reduce noise and, at the same time, provide a degree of privacy. Alternatively, hang fabric dividers as an effective barrier between a bed and the adjacent zone. This is a simple device that focuses attention on the bed in the sleeping zone while concealing it from

left and above
A metal sleeping platform provides an inventive sleeping area in an attic apartment. When positioning such a platform, consider the amount of space that will remain above and below.

This is a critical measurement that affects ease of use and comfort. Ideally, allow enough height above the bed for standing room on the platform. The area beneath the platform can be used as a storage space.

the rest of an open-plan environment. If space is limited, dedicating a separate area to sleeping is not always an option. Combining a sleeping zone with a different yet compatible activity is one solution, and is a good way to make the most of the available space. Alternatively, inserting a mezzanine level or sleeping platform will provide an extra level that is independent from the main space.

A mezzanine level effectively adds a new floor, or part of a new floor, to a double height space. It is a complex structural undertaking requiring careful planning. The size and scope of a mezzanine is dependent upon the overall dimensions of your space. If extra space is essential to accommodate several individual requirements, such as a guest bedroom, or a separate work area, consider inserting more than one mezzanine, or adding ones at different levels. Include independent access to each level. However, even if it is possible to insert an mezzanine,

it is counter-productive to do so if one will compromise a general sense of openness and light in the interior.

Adding a small sleeping platform, just large enough for a bed, reading light and alarm clock, is a simpler undertaking. However, although very different in size and complexity, both options offer an opportunity to introduce a new structural and visual dimension to an open-plan environment. A new level provides two-way views, both out of and into the new area, frees up space beneath, and offers a sense of separation without losing a vital connection with the main space.

Try to place a mezzanine or sleeping platform in a position where it will enjoy a special view of the interior, or has access to a window with attractive views. Bear in mind the importance of ventilation. If it is possible, insert a skylight above the new level to increase the flow of light and air, or position the new level where it will receive direct light

below The imposing dimensions of a former period sitting room provide sufficient height for this space-saving solution. A compact sleeping platform fits above a kitchen area, and is accessed via a movable ladder. The platform overlooks the dining and sitting area beyond.

from an existing window. Nothing can compete with the good effects of waking up to natural light.

If space is at a premium, removing or moving a bed when not in use liberates a considerable amount of space and adds flexibility. A dual-function zone, perhaps combining sleeping and working, or sleeping and a child's play area, allows you to put the space to good use during the day. Mobility – perhaps a worktable on wheels, or lightweight plastic storage boxes for toys – will facilitate the crossover. Assembling and dismantling anything on a day-to-day basis is unrealistic and too time-consuming.

Fold-up beds, where the bed lifts vertically into a storage box, are clever space-saving devices that facilitate flexible sleeping arrangements. They are ideal for a small space and also offer useful back-up accommodation. The key to fold-up efficiency is a lightweight mechanism for ease of use. Beware of labour-intensive manual designs – these soon become a chore as an everyday option. One possible disadvantage of a fold-up system is finding adequate storage for bed linen when the bed is out of the way. One solution is to build in a cupboard beside or above the folding bed box. Another option is a bed on wheels that can swivel into place or out of the way as needed. This will not clear the same amount of space as a fold-up bed, but it will shift the emphasis of a zone from one specific activity to make way for an alternative.

below In a sequence of simple movements, a fold-up bed swings vertically into a cupboard. Fixing shelves into the back of the recess provides extra storage for clothes and bed linen.

left and above What appears to be a cupboard in fact conceals a roomy double bed. When space is at a premium, a fold-up bed is an ingenious solution. The easy, gliding mechanism of a fold-up system requires minimum effort to operate, and allows you to hide away the bed when not in use. Fold-ups are ideal for dual-function areas, as they free up valuable space for a different activity, allowing a sleeping area to double as a work or play zone.

new york loft space

LOW-KEY LOFT SPACE

In this light, white and functional New York loft space, a textile designer combines a place to live and work with ease and efficiency. Loose cotton covers on armchairs, a long sociable dining table, lively dogs and sleeping cats, and bundles of fresh flowers project an overall sense of welcome, calm and comfort. Yet this tranquil living space is also the centre of a buzzing international textile business.

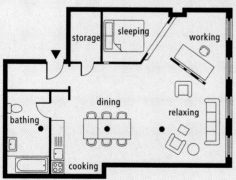

Formerly a sewing factory in New York's Tribeca district, this space is a low-tech conversion with exposed surface power conduits and low-maintenance scrub-down floors and worktops. Four south-facing windows ranged along the length of one wall provide light for the whole space. The interior retains a sense of openness and light while providing different degrees of separation for living and working. It is a triumph of simplicity and invention.

The main living area, a logical sequence of everyday activities from kitchen to dining to sitting, extends almost the full length of one side of the loft, following a line of decorative cast-iron columns. Along the opposite side of the space are the sleeping and work areas. The sleeping area is a square box just large enough for a double bed, set one step up from the main space. Completely open on one side, with views across the living and work areas to the windows beyond, it enjoys plenty of natural light. A diagonal step running the full width of the opening adds an essential extra triangle of floor space at the bottom of the bed, providing a place to step into. Simple voile curtains pull across the opening to enclose the whole area. The change in floor level and the voile screen signal a different territory, a retreat from the buzzy world beyond.

The work zone projects a very different dynamic. A fixed floor-to-ceiling panel, studded with rectangular glass

floor plan Access from a communal stairway leads directly into the main living zone. Three cast-iron pillars run down one side of the interior, with four south-facing windows along the end wall. An internal opening between the cooking and bathing zones allows natural light to penetrate the full length of the loft.

opposite above
Aligning the work
table behind a fixed
divider effectively
conceals office
equipment.
this page Voile
curtains and a change
in floor level separate
the sleeping area
from the main space.

insets, is set diagonally across one corner of the space to create a semi-separate work area. The divider is an ingenious solution, allowing easy access but also providing a degree of separation. It defines the compact work area, yet at the same time promotes a sense of openness, light and connection.

Open shelving and a folding tray table provide storage for office supplies and papers. A work table on castors sits directly behind the divider, home to the owner's computer. An inspiration board, fabric swatches, postcards and knick-knacks adorn the space, adding colour and detail. All in all, this is a compact, efficient work area, practically invisible from the living area opposite.

Developing the space is an on-going project, with the best ideas, like the sleeping platform and divider, evolving out of the owner's determination to fit all the requirements of a busy life into an imperfect space. The simplicity of the all-white aesthetic unifies any imperfections and quirky details and adds to an overall sense of space and light.

opposite The main living space is light and white, with the kitchen, eating and relaxing zones down one side. The work zone is set up behind a diagonal screen, which conceals it without separating it from the main space.

right Easy-access open shelving, base units and a tile splashback focus the kitchen zone along one wall. The long table for food preparation, eating and working also provides a drop zone for shopping bags.

working

WHETHER YOU DESIGNATE A SEPARATE AREA FOR WORK OR COMBINE ACTIVITIES IN A MULTI-FUNCTIONAL ZONE, GOOD ORGANIZATION AND PLENTY OF FLEXIBILITY WILL HAVE A BIG IMPACT ON YOUR EFFICIENCY AND ENJOYMENT.

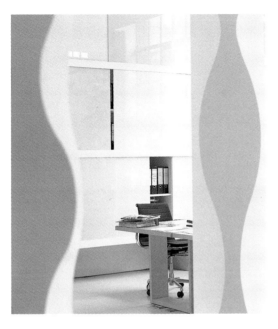

Investing time and effort in creating an enjoyable, comfortable and efficient working place is essential for health and well-being. If working and living in the same space is a permanent arrangement, then it is important to acknowledge this with a commitment to finding a work space that enjoys a source of natural light and fresh air. This can be as simple as an area beside a window that you can screen off from other zones, or as expansive as an entire mezzanine level for use as a home office. The big advantage of a permanent work space is that it allows you to leave everything where it is from one day to the next without having to tidy all your things away at the end of the day.

Setting up a work place in an awkward or badly lit area in an attempt to impinge as little as possible on your living space is a mistake. It may seem like a good short-term option, but will soon develop into an unhealthy long-term one. If you work from home, equipment, paperwork and space requirements are likely

opposite A combination of hanging paper banners and a decorative folding screen effectively separate a work zone from a main living area.

above left and right Glossy perspex panels set on runners screen deep shelves and slide along to provide easy access to files, but conceal all when the space reverts to domestic use in the evening.

to increase, not decrease, so finding an area that can only just accommodate a working zone is impractical, as it makes no provision for future developments.

If space is at a premium, then a dual-function area will offer you greater flexibility and freedom than an entirely separate work zone. A dual-function area does require a degree of transfer from one activity to another, but this can be as simple as wheeling a work table into the centre of a space. In theory, any area that is not in use during the working day is a possible option for a work zone. For example, if you can easily convert a light and open relaxing area into a place to work, this is a good option. If the conversion requires a minor compromise to an otherwise efficient arrangement, such as storing files in another area, then the benefits are greater than the inconvenience. However, if you require frequent access to the files then this level of compromise may be unworkable as an everyday arrangement.

Consider access to your work area. It is a good idea to choose somewhere out of the way of general household traffic and to devise a degree of separation from the overall space. If you share a household with children who are at home during the

far left A small desk tucked into a quiet corner may be all you need to house your laptop, pay bills and keep up with your correspondence.
left Reduce the visual impact and office-like effect of an extensive filing system by hiding files behind sliding panels, paper screens or simple roller blinds.

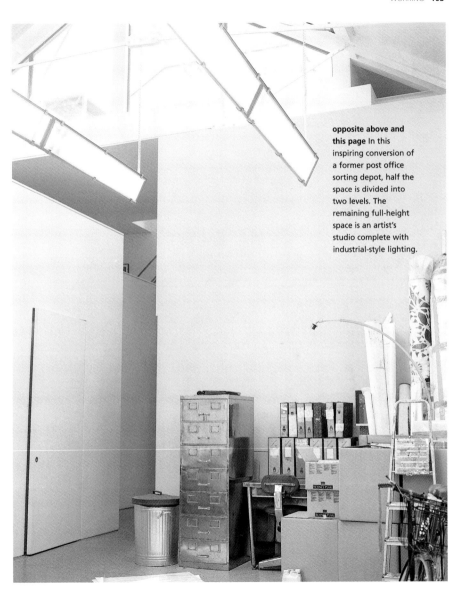

opposite above and this page In this inspiring conversion of a former post office sorting depot, half the space is divided into two levels. The remaining full-height space is an artist's studio complete with industrial-style lighting.

day, taking over an area they like to use and denying them access will be problematic. If possible, work somewhere less central or popular – it will create less conflict. Alternatively, invest in mobile furniture and storage, and plan where to work on a day-to-day basis.

Good ergonomics play a key role in determining and designing an ideal work environment and are vital for health and well-being. If you spend several hours a day sitting down to type or draw, constantly repeating a sequence of similar movements, then it is essential to invest in a supportive, adjustable chair and an adequate table or drawing board. If you

frequently refer to a filing system, easy access is vital. Depending on the type of work you do, a kitchen table can provide a work area. However, the height of a domestic table is incompatible with an ergonomic position for typing, so this situation is not suitable for long-term keyboard use.

If you work on a computer, consider the position of the screen in relation to direct light. Avoid the glare of a back-lit screen or the mirror-effect caused by direct light on a screen. As light levels change during the day, modulate them with blinds. Supplementary task lighting is an essential back-up to natural light; it is

opposite left In a compact New York apartment, an open-plan living and sleeping area undergoes a daily tranformation to a work zone for the two architect owners. **opposite right** The space is full of clever details, such as a wall of floor-to-ceiling wooden panels that slide to one side to reveal flat-folding drawing boards. **left** The wooden panels open and overlap to reveal two drawing boards that fold up from the walls. The 1950s bar stools double up as office seating.

not advisable to work long hours in an area without either. Setting up a work space in your home can require a big expenditure, especially if you need specialist equipment, so invest in flexible free-standing storage solutions and key items that can adapt to a review of your working habits or changes in circumstances. You can also take them with you when you move. Typical office-style furniture tends to look alien in an open-plan living space, so if you want to use this kind of furniture, it is best to screen it in some way. Traditional utilitarian metal filing cabinets and work tables look less unforgiving but lack the

slick efficiency of new products. Check out creative and ergonomic alternatives in contemporary furniture showrooms or look in architectural or design magazines for details of suppliers.

If you do not need specialist storage systems, then use standard storage boxes and files. Avoid the children's playroom effect of colourful plastic bins and use metal, wood, cardboard or clear plastic containers. Low-level storage, such as boxes beneath a worktable or a bench unit with a lift-up lid, is less obtrusive than high-level shelving, wall units or cabinets. And custom-built furniture can maximize and individualize a space.

new york recycled

CASE STUDY 5

LOFT SPACE WITH A CONTAINER TRUCK

Recycling a container truck as a device to divide an open-plan interior is an extraordinary concept. Yet it provides an efficient, practical and flexible solution. Installing it in an ex-commercial unit in midtown Manhattan imposes a powerful industrial aesthetic on a basic structural shell, unifies an irregular space and defines and sub-divides a multi-functional environment.

FLAMMABLE
GAS

PULL
HERE

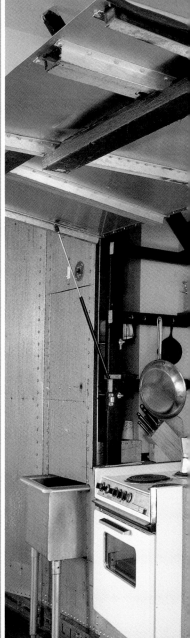

A photographer and theatrical set designer took on this ex-commercial unit with the intention of developing a versatile open-plan living and working environment. The challenge of a scheme like this, as with many open-plan multi-functional environments, is a complex question of how to organize the space, prioritize and integrate activities, and incorporate adequate provisions for separation. In this case, for a creative New York couple, a private sleeping area on view to visiting clients is unacceptable, whereas a large worktable hijacking much of the main living area is fine.

The space itself, a basic rectangle with an add-on square at the back, suggests a logical division into front-of-house and back-of-house activities. Positioning the everyday appliances, like the shower, kitchen sink and cooker, along a single axis also

above Using the container-truck divider to house a television and video underlines its
involvement in the day-to-day activities of the loft.
right In the kitchen area, different
sections of the truck siding flip up to reveal appliances, cooking and food preparation zones.

simplifies division and separation. For the architects, establishing this single axis became the starting point for an inventive installation in keeping with their commitment to recycling industrial cast-offs. The aluminium siding of a container truck has been installed as a divider, and effectively intersects the loft on a diagonal, drawing a dramatic and assertive line between the public and private areas.

The aluminium siding is cut into a number of different moving sections, all of which flip up, pivot or rotate to reveal different functions. The sections look rough and heavy, yet the mechanisms that control them are precise and efficient, so lifting and opening individual sections does not require any exertion. Indeed, the ease of operation positively promotes flexibility and immediate manipulation of space.

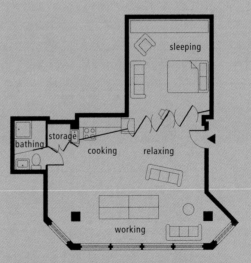

floor plan The space is a rough rectangle with windows along one side, next to the relaxing and work areas. Two add-on squares provide a sleeping area at back and a bathing area to one side. The truck siding divides the space diagonally, extending from beside the entrance through to the bathing zone.

A wooden frame props up the aluminium siding like a billboard and supports horizontal aluminium beams running along the top and bottom of the siding. In the kitchen, two flip-up sections conceal the cooking and food preparation areas, with a cupboard door over the sink. Operating independently or together, the sections provide various combinations or degrees of openness. With all the sections shut, an abstract line-up of appliances protrudes from the aluminium. However, thanks to frequent use, all or part of the kitchen usually remains open, providing vibrant background colour.

Separating the living and sleeping areas, three independent sections spin like swing doors, offering easy access and multiple variations of openness. Changing the position of the middle section also controls the angle of a built-in video and television. When the section is closed, the

television faces the main living area. When the section is fully open, it is possible to watch television from the bed.

The front-of-house area is a flexible living and working area, with the emphasis firmly on working. The main focus of the space is one large workstation on wheels that contains everything relating to work. In theory the table can be moved, but in practice it remains in situ, the centre of activity.

opposite The side of the container truck divides the loft diagonally into front-of-house working and relaxing areas and back-of-house sleeping zones. The kitchen area and appliances are part and parcel of the diagonal axis itself.

above left Recycling old commercial filing cabinets and metal lockers provides an ingenious wall of storage in the sleeping area.

above right When the panel containing the television swings round, the screen is visible from the bed.

open-plan
essentials

dividing I lighting I storing

ONE OF THE MAIN CONCERNS OF LIVING IN AN
OPEN-PLAN HOME IS FINDING WAYS TO SUBDIVIDE
IT EFFECTIVELY. DIVIDERS ALLOW YOU TO SEPARATE
AREAS WITHOUT COMPROMISING THE OVERALL
SENSE OF SPACE AND LIGHT DISTRIBUTION.

dividing

There are many different kinds of dividers, but they roughly fall into two groups. The first group consists of permanent dividers, which are fixed, such as a glass-brick wall, or adjustable, such as sliding panels or sections of wall. The second group is made up of freestanding dividers, such as screens, that can be moved around at will. Choose dividers that will meet your requirements in terms of space, flexibility, overall aesthetics and cost-efficiency.

When assessing your requirements, consider the way you use your space. Do you need to subdivide the space daily, perhaps alternating between an open-plan relaxing zone and a separate work area, or will you divide it less frequently? Will you be happy with lightweight divisions between sleeping and bathing areas, or is a more substantial partition needed? Do you require complete isolation in any part of your space – for a child's sleeping area, for example? Using dividers to change the mood of the space is another possibility, allowing you to transform an open living space into an intimate one, or introduce a new configuration of space to suit a change in season or activity.

Permanent divisions can compromise versatility, especially in more compact spaces. However, there are advantages to fixed dividers. A low-level partition wall between public and private areas, for instance, can incorporate the services and utilities for

opposite A simple wooden frame supports perspex panels set in a curve to divide living and sleeping areas and provide storage.
above left and centre Inexpensive curtain track hung with plastic sheeting separates a sleeping area from the main living zone.
above right Simple muslin drapes conceal a wall of storage in an open-plan living and bathing area, and provide a degree of separation between different zones.

below A change in floor covering can act as an effective divider. Here, a change from wood to carpeting maps out different zones within a loft.

a kitchen or bathing area, or provide generous storage space on both sides of the wall. To retain a sense of openness, leave openings either side of a fixed partition, or a gap between the top of the panel and the ceiling. If a floor-to-ceiling partition is essential for insulation or privacy, use opaque glass or glass bricks or knock through internal windows to boost light distribution and create a sense of connection throughout the space.

If you want to install fixed dividers yet retain optimum flexibility, opt for moving, sliding, swivelling, pivoting or folding panels. These will enable you to carve up a space into several different areas without compromising versatility or provision for privacy, allowing the interior to revert to maximum openness when desired. Where the panels are stored when not in use, and how easy they are to operate, are both important considerations. When not fully extended, sliding panels usually cover a section of wall, overlap each other, or slot away neatly into a recess in a wall. Pivoting or folding panels usually close up and fold away flat in a recess in a wall, like giant shutters. Both sliding and pivoting panels require recessed metal tracks set into the floor and ceiling to support them. Recessed tracks in the floor are not always strictly necessary, but they do add stability. For panels that slot into a wall recess, fit retractable handles on the reveal.

opposite below left
This kitchen offers
many levels of
enclosure and
division, with flip-
down panels to hide
work surfaces, sliding
panels to shut it off
and a roller blind.
opposite below right
Panels with
retractable handles
on recessed runners
allow a frequent and
easy reconfiguration
of space.

left In a spacious
New York loft,
moving dividers
facilitate frequent
changeovers from
an open-plan
mezzanine to two
sleeping enclosures
and a bathing area.
above A two-way
opening in an
opaque glass panel
cleverly screens off
a bathing area
without blocking
natural light.

Mobile screens can perform a similar function to built-in panels, but they give you the freedom to reconfigure space in any way at any time. Japanese paper and wood screens, folding wooden screens and hospital-style fabric and metal screens all provide different degrees of separation and are appropriate to different styles of interior. Alternatively, make your own screens with MDF panels and flat hinges. Or, for a quick solution, throw fabric over a mobile clothes rail. Large paintings, a sheet of perspex, fabric or paper banners, strings of beads or metal chains hanging from ceiling rails or hooks will all effectively demarcate space and will combat a lack of variation in a featureless interior.

Decoration and furnishings can also indicate a change in area or activity, effectively dividing a single space into several different zones. A change in floor covering, from concrete paving slabs to wooden floorboards, or rubber tiles to woollen carpet or rugs, can help differentiate between a hard-working public area and a relaxing private one. Arrange furniture, especially key items like sofas and tables, in social groupings to define different activity areas. And use large pieces of furniture like book cases or cabinets to divide space. Colour can also unify or divide a space. Paint a wall or use a single-colour rug or a series of chairs in identical or co-ordinating colours to draw attention to a specific grouping or divide an open-plan scheme visually.

above left A narrow bathing area has been slotted in between sleeping and working zones and is separated from the living area by a sheet of clear glass covered with a sliding plastic panel that provides essential privacy.

opposite This sophisticated track system supports lightweight corrugated-plastic panels that divide private and public areas without blocking light in a potentially dark and gloomy semi-underground space.

LIGHT IS A VITAL ELEMENT IN OPEN-PLAN
INTERIORS, IMAGINATIVE INSTALLATIONS CAN
OPTIMIZE A SENSE OF SPACE AND UNITY,
PROVIDE A FOCUS FOR DIFFERENT ACTIVITY
ZONES AND DEMARCATE THE OVERALL SPACE.

lighting

Looking at the way natural light affects different parts of a space is a good starting point for deciding how to organize an open-plan environment. It makes sense to devote the best-lit areas to key zones, such as relaxing or cooking and eating. Any area with a good supply of light will always be a welcoming space.

If it is possible and cost-efficient to reconfigure your space in any way, it is worth increasing the amount of incoming light by inserting new windows or skylights or enlarging existing ones. Removing or reducing the size of internal walls, inserting internal windows or, in a space on more than one level, removing part of a floor to create a double-height opening, will all have a dramatic effect on light distribution and will enhance dark areas by providing access to natural light. White walls, ceilings or floors and glass walls or floors, especially on mezzanine levels or galleries, will improve light levels. Shiny surfaces such as glass, metal and perspex will also animate a space by reflecting light.

Modulating the amount of incoming light is easy. Window treatments such as roller blinds, Venetian blinds or curtains are all inexpensive solutions and offer privacy when needed. To diffuse light or screen an unappealing view, hang paper banners or roller blinds at the window. If it is necessary to block out light completely, fit shutters or black-out blinds.

above left Roller blinds modulate the incoming light at expansive windows. **above centre and right** Venetian blinds control light levels and can black out the space when darkness is required. **opposite** In an ex-industrial space with large metal-frame windows, a banner of tracing paper hanging from a metal pole diffuses light and adds an element of privacy.

Use artifical light to supplement natural light and to add versatility and variation to a space. Artificial lighting falls into four groups: ambient, task, accent and information. Ambient lighting is general background lighting that throws light over a wide area. Task lighting illuminates one area to aid a specific task or activity. Accent lighting can highlight an architectural feature or decorative object. Information lighting helps you move around a space safely, illuminating a change in floor-level, for example. A combination of all four types will create a comfortable, user-friendly environment.

Different light sources and fittings create different effects. Halogen lighting is cool and modern, while tungsten is warm and mellow. Fluorescent lighting can create similar effects to both halogen and tungsten, and has the added bonus of being ecologically friendly. There is an enormous range of different fittings available. The ones you choose will depend on personal preference, but it is important to make sure the fittings will do exactly what you want them to. Central ceiling lights create a pool of light and can indicate a key area, such as a relaxing zone. Add other lights, such as floor and table lamps, to enliven the scheme. Spotlights throw a strong pool of light and can usually be adjusted to suit different uses and activities. Track and barewire lighting carry miniature spotlights, which can be individually

opposite below left In a workshop conversion in Paris, a decorative central light adorns a simple eating area.
opposite below centre This versatile aluminium fitting can be used as a spotlight or an uplighter.
opposite below right Minimalist in feel, track and barewire lighting offers a flexible alternative to fixed spotlights.

below Adjustable shiny chrome wall lights are used here as uplighters to bounce light off a white ceiling and illuminate a small reading area.
right Recycling a hospital light as a task light in this kitchen area is in keeping with the large scale of the space, the industrial feel and the owner's heavy-duty catering equipment.

opposite A mix of fluorescent tube lighting concealed behind sliding plastic panels and a sculptural Tom Dixon floor light animate and add colour to a pared-down interior.

right Decorative floor lights provide illumination but also bring interest and atmosphere to an interior.
below A simple detail like matching lights and paint shades transforms three simple wall recesses into a focal point in a low-key relaxation zone.

angled or adjusted, on tensioned cables. Uplighters and downlighters reflect light in a particular direction. Uplighters bounce light off the walls and ceiling and provide soft, diffused, illumination, while downlighters cast a pool of light downwards, like a spotlight. There are many types of uplighter on the market, while downlighters are often recessed in the ceiling.

The arrangement and combination of different types of lighting can unify or divide a space just as effectively as any structural dividers by creating different effects, illuminating an overall space or focusing on a specific area or activity. In a multi-functional area such as a relaxing zone, fit ambient lights with dimmers and provide selective accent or decorative lighting for contrast. Use task lighting to signal areas set aside for activities such as reading or working on the computer. In a kitchen or work area, it is essential to provide sufficient task lighting.

Installing new lighting can be disruptive, so wiring in fittings, power points and switches should take place in conjunction with any other building work. Calculate how many electrical sockets and light fittings you require for different activities or zones. In a space with a large floor area, fit sockets in the floor for maximum flexibility. A qualified electrician will be able to give you advice, assess your electrical infrastructure and let you know if your current system needs updating or extending.

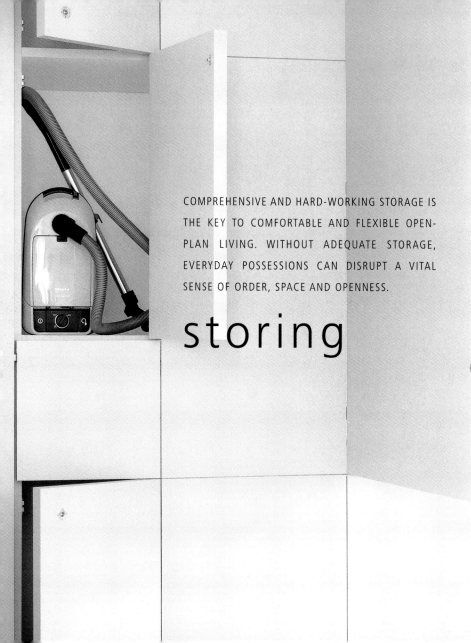

COMPREHENSIVE AND HARD-WORKING STORAGE IS THE KEY TO COMFORTABLE AND FLEXIBLE OPEN-PLAN LIVING. WITHOUT ADEQUATE STORAGE, EVERYDAY POSSESSIONS CAN DISRUPT A VITAL SENSE OF ORDER, SPACE AND OPENNESS.

storing

opposite A large square 'pod' in the centre of an open-plan interior contains bathing and sleeping areas as well as ample storage space.

Providing adequate provision for storage is the key to organizing an open-plan environment. Storage solutions can resolve basic issues such as where to keep clothing and kitchen items or conceal bulky pieces of equipment such as televisions, washing machines and computers. In a multi-functional environment, good storage will help you to retain flexibility, visual simplicity and freedom of choice.

It is often more practical to devote a substantial proportion of space to storage to ease pressure on a general living space, rather than maintain maximum space at the expense of comfort and practicality. In Japanese homes, where space is a critical issue, one-third of every household is taken up by storage. Although this may seem like a disproportionate amount of storage to living space, sufficient storage can make an open-plan home more flexible, allowing for simple and efficient changeovers between different activities, such as relaxing or working or sleeping.

Be realistic about storage requirements in an open-plan interior. Creating a sense of space and order is

above This low-level storage unit offers a variety of open cubes, shelving and drawers. Units like this look unobtrusive and orderly and accommodate large amounts of essential equipment.
left Rows of identical cardboard boxes neatly stacked in a basic industrial-style shelving system provides an easily accessible home for papers, photos and out-of-season clothes.

not always about finding a home for every single possession, but about living with what is essential and functional. Edit your possessions and select a capsule collection of kitchenware, entertainment equipment, clothing and other key items, then design and plan your storage solutions accordingly.

The basic options for different kinds of storage are either structural systems, such as a dividing wall with built-in shelves or cupboards, fixed systems, such as wall-mounted shelving or modular units, or freestanding storage. All of these options can provide open storage for display or conceal items in some way.

Many contemporary architects incorporate built-in storage in structural features, using perimeter or dividing walls to conceal streamlined floor-to-ceiling cupboards that can accommodate the essential clutter of everyday life. Built-in storage can also make use of irregular structural details or otherwise unused space in a way that ready-made storage items cannot, by tucking a custom-made clothes rail or drawer unit beneath a sloping ceiling, for example, or fitting drawers into stair treads. Fixed storage, such as wall-mounted modular systems, presents plenty of functional options for both concealed storage and display space. Freestanding and mobile storage is highly flexible, as it can be moved around from area to area as needed.

Different areas require different storage provisions. In a kitchen area, the emphasis is on quick and easy access to key items. Store utensils that are in frequent use within an arm's length of the work area. Ideally, keep pots and pans next to the

above right Sliding plastic panels conceal a compact wedge-shaped storage area, which extends the full length of an small open-plan apartment

right Chunky open shelves fixed in front of a window create a focal point in a long, narrow kitchen area. The shelves provide storage space but do not block the light.

left In a compact space, clever details, like this sleek streamlined metal holder for a roll of kitchen paper, make the most of the available space. **below left** This precise made-to-measure storage unit has been wedged into a tiny gap in a small kitchen zone. It brings a bright splash of colour to the kitchen area, and utilizes what would otherwise be wasted space.

below Functional laboratory-style units, a stainless steel splashback and suspended glass shelving optimize the available space in a New York kitchen with an industrial aesthetic.

oven or hob, fresh vegetables adjacent to the food-preparation area and kitchenware in close proximity to the dishwasher for easy unloading. When planning storage for a kitchen area, bear in mind that whatever you install is likely to be visible from the main living area, if not from every part of the space, so flexible dividers such as flip-up or sliding panels or roller blinds that pull down to screen the kitchen area will allow you to conceal clutter. Choose a combination of freestanding items and open shelving or fitted wall and base units, depending on your requirements. Low-level mobile storage units are space-efficient additions to any kitchen area and can be stored under work surfaces and wheeled out when they are needed.

A flexible storage system is essential in a multi-functioning living space, especially if you live as a family or with several other people. Leaving all your possessions in full view can look cluttered and untidy, yet if everything is hidden away an area can look sterile and anonymous. Aim to reveal a few items that represent different activities, but to conceal large CD or book collections. Sliding panels, roller blinds or mobile screens can hide electrical equipment or a wall of books, yet still allow easy access to the items. In a living area, storage options include wall-mounted units, low-level shelving or cabinets, freestanding cupboards or modular cube systems. A mobile computer desk for your laptop or an entertainment system on a wheeled

trolley is a flexible storage option, as it can be pushed out into a central position when needed, then stashed away in a different area afterwards.

As well as storage items designed for the domestic market, there are many alternatives available from commercial or trade suppliers, such as catering, retail, office and medical storage systems. The large scale and utilitarian design of these products means that they fit in well with ex-industrial interiors. And on a practical level, items originally made to industrial or commercial standards provide greater storage capacity than their domestic counterparts. However, a filing cabinet or airline locker takes up lots of space, so avoid overwhelming a compact scheme with over-sized furniture.

opposite left A glossy red trolley with drawers acts as a mobile storage centre for CDs, DVDs, a telephone and directories.

opposite centre Using second-hand catering equipment for storage is in keeping with the scale and industrial aesthetic of this kitchen area.

opposite right A versatile folding trolley stores away flat when not in use and provides an extra work surface in the kitchen area at a moment's notice.

above left This inventive custom-made storage system utilizes the wasted space beneath stair treads by using them as a chest of drawers.

above centre A metal bucket hanging from a rope and pulley can be lowered to give access to household items or raised so it is out of view.

above right Clever design maximizes the potential of this mini closet. It contains a small fold-down ironing board and pull-out clothes rail.

a practical
approach

heating | insulation | ventilation | noise | assessing change

Creating an ideal living environment is a matter of individual taste, although fresh air and warmth are vital for everyone's well-being. And while simple joys like opening a window on a spring morning or lighting a stove in winter are rewarding emotional and physical pleasures, even the most elemental domestic space will benefit from some degree of ventilation and heating.

In an open-plan home, devising effective service systems requires precise planning and assessment. As a general guide, when choosing new service systems or upgrading, adapting or extending existing ones, consider all aspects of performance, the cost of installation and level of disruption, running costs, aesthetics, flexibility and maintenance.

Many conventional domestic systems work well in open-plan apartments and conversions built to standard proportions. Yet the proportions and expansiveness of some conversions, especially former non-domestic spaces like schools or light-industrial factories, often require a combination of high performance products and systems.

Heating In general, domestic heating is usually supplied via convenient, cost-effective central heating systems or by a series of independent heaters.

Central heating systems are either wet or dry systems. Wet systems heat water in a boiler using gas, electricity, solid fuel, wood or oil and distribute the hot water via pipes to radiators, convector radiators and underfloor heating pipes. Individual thermostats can adjust the temperature on different radiators and floor and wall convector radiators, whereas a single thermostat sets the temperature for all trench convector radiators and underfloor heating pipes. Wet systems usually heat the domestic hot water supply too.

Dry systems use gas, electricity or oil-fuelled heaters to warm air and distribute it through a system of ducts, grilles and convector heaters. A central thermostat controls air temperature throughout the system. However, with an additional cooling coil, dry systems can distribute cold air as well as hot, which is a big bonus in hot weather. Heating ducts transmit sound as well as air, so avoid placing machines or equipment next to vents or outlets. Both wet and dry heating systems take moisture out of the air so it is essential to keep fresh air circulating. Humidifiers and dehumidifiers can adjust air-moisture content. Alternatively, a simple bowl of water on the floor, Japanese-style, will restore moisture to dry air – drop in a pebble for visual interest.

Radiators, exclusive to wet systems, are available in every size, style and colour imaginable, and can be fixed to walls or stand on floors. They are usually made from steel, although cast iron and aluminium models are also available. Different configurations of coils and fins deliver different amounts of heat, so calculate performance in conjunction with aesthetics.

Radiators are efficient, economical, easy to control and require little maintenance.

Bear in mind that if you have an expansive open-plan environment with radiators attached to the perimeter walls, heat can take some time to radiate to the centre of the space. An electric ceiling fan, or series of fans, can help circulation Alternatively, you could find a way of fixing a radiator (or radiators) in the centre of the space – perhaps using an existing architectural feature like a column. Incorporating an additional heating source, such as a stove or underfloor heating system will also prevent potential cold spots.

Good air circulation around each radiator ensures maximum heat radiation, so try not to restrict air flow with big items of furniture like sofas or book cases. Depending on the available wall space, this may present a problem.

Radiators often occupy premium wall space, which can leave big pieces of furniture and paintings with no place to go. Work out a floorplan before installation to avoid any conflicts. Finally, resist the temptation to use radiators for drying wet clothes, as this will create a build-up of condensation.

Convector radiators blow hot or cold air and run on electricity or are connected to either wet or dry heating systems. Compact and unobtrusive, with grill fascias, they can be fixed to walls or ceilings or, ideally, fitted in trenches in flooring, beneath cabinets or in stair treads and skirting boards. For visual simplicity and to reduce the dust-trap effect of grill fascias, install convector radiators in a recess or box and conceal them with metal or wooden ventilation panels that are in keeping with the architectural style of the space.

opposite above right Vertical radiators are highly visible, so stick to simple colours and designs. Fitting them in a recess or niche makes them less obtrusive.
above left These basic, low-budget radiators are low-key and unobtrusive.
above centre If you have the space, original cast-iron radiators provide substantial levels of heat. Sand-blast to remove paint and seal them to keep them free from rust.
above right A trench radiator with metal grille delivers heat all along a line of sliding plastic panels that separate living and sleeping areas.

top and above
Fresh air is vital.
Make sure all your
windows open and
consider installing
a ventilation system
to boost air
circulation. Always
fit extractors in
cooking areas.

Underfloor heating pipes, unlike convector heaters in trenches, will heat up an entire floor. This is invisible heating with a high comfort factor. Most underfloor heating pipes run off wet systems, circulating hot water through thermoplastic pipes set in concrete or an underfloor cavity. Installation involves pulling up the whole floor, so this option is a big commitment, a big effort and a big expense. However, the water circulating through the system is not as hot as the water that circulates in a wet radiator system, so underfloor heating is cost-efficient to use. And if run in combination with a radiator system, it is possible to recycle some of the warm water. All-round good insulation is essential to minimize heat loss.

Stoves that run on gas, wood or solid fuel generate a great deal of heat and provide a striking focal point in an interior. They are capable of running a central heating system, but are most commonly used to heat hot water and boost central heating systems. Stoves are high maintenance, requiring regular cleaning and fresh fuel every few hours (except gas stoves), so are more labour intensive on a day-to-day basis. Strict safety precautions apply for flue maintenance and installation, and it is advisable to check with your local authority about any fuel restrictions.

Other forms of heating worth considering include solar systems, which are ecologically-friendly, simple to install,

require a good supply of sunshine, access to a roof to fit solar panels or sheets and a back-up system for when sunshine is not on the menu. Freestanding electric storage heaters provide low-cost background heating in a big space but they take up a lot of room. Electric fans, electric element heaters or gas storage-bottle heaters are all adequate sources of additional localized heat.

Insulation Generating heat is only one part of the equation – reducing your heat loss and fuel consumption is just as important. Practical DIY insulating measures like attaching draught excluders to doors and windows, insulating roof space and lagging pipes, hot water tanks and storage cisterns will all significantly reduce heat loss. Professional measures like insulating cavity walls, floors and ceilings and double-glazing your windows will also maximize efficiency. However, it takes a little time to see a return on your investment in terms of savings on your fuel bills. If you are planning a total refit of your home, or other major building work, incorporating these measures at the same time will be less disruptive and less expensive.

Ventilation Good ventilation is essential to prevent a build-up of moisture and condensation, which creates an unhealthy living environment and can damage the fabric of a building. Opening windows is the simplest way to keep fresh air circulating. You could also install ceiling fans in large spaces or areas away from open windows to ensure an air current. Fit ventilation fans to expel stale air and draw in fresh air. In compliance with standard public health and safety regulations, fit extractor fans in cooking and bathing areas – they will remove excessive moisture and potential condensation and eliminate smells to maintain a healthy, pleasant atmosphere.

Noise One inevitable effect of introducing effective heating and ventilation systems is a general increase in ambient noise levels. Incorporating good insulation in the fabric of the building will significantly reduce the amount of noise entering from outside, while insulating pipes, boilers, cisterns and ducts, including at points of entry and exit, should also significantly reduce amounts of internal noise.

Wherever possible, isolate and insulate domestic machines such as tumble dryers and washing machines in a purpose-built utility cupboard or alcove. Other possible solutions are a combination, or possibly compromise, of planning and design decisions and individual aesthetics. For example, in simple architectural interiors with bare floors and walls, sound will echo and multiply in ratio to the number of people in the space. Using thick, sound-absorbing rugs to define different areas of activity and hanging fabric roller blinds will help to alleviate the echo problem and cut down on noise transference. However, a degree of ambient noise and noise transference is, unfortunately, a factor of one-space living.

Assessing change Reducing heat loss, fuel consumption and noise pollution and maintaining a clean and healthy living environment are all ecologically-friendly objectives. Deficient, outdated services are inefficient and uneconomical, so it seems a logical step to replace them with more up-to-date efficient systems. Whatever level of change or installation you envisage, get professional advice to assess what already exists, what is possible and what products and systems are relevant to your requirements. Even simple projects like upgrading the existing radiators on a wet system may require an upgrade in your boiler as well. Likewise with electricity – it is essential to check electrical systems are safe and capable of supporting everyday requirements. New appliances may require new circuitry.

As a general rule, the simpler the layout of a system, the fewer the potential problems. Keep a plan of piping, ducts and wiring to assist with any future maintenance and servicing. Quick access to stopcocks and circuit breakers is essential in an emergency – ideally install them in an area with easy access, like an understairs cupboard or behind a panel in the wall or floor, and clearly label all the pipes, switches and stopcocks in view.

stockists and suppliers

HELP AND ADVICE

Architects Registration Board
73 Hallam Street
London W1N 6EE
020 7580 5861
www.arb.org.uk
The Architects Registration Board maintains a register of qualified architects.

The British Institute of Architectural Technologists
397 City Road
London EC1V 1NE
020 7278 2206
www.biat.org.uk
Architectural Technologists are concerned with the technical performance of buildings and can supply technical drawings and specify suitable materials for building projects. The institute publishes an annual directory of practices that have a BIAT member as a partner or director.

The Building Centre
26 Store Street
London WC1E 7BT
020 7692 4040
www.buildingcentre.co.uk
The Building Centre Bookshop stocks a wide range of useful publications covering architecture, surveying, engineering, building contractors, manufacturers, suppliers and trade associations.

The Building Centre Guideline
09065 161 136
This helpful telephone enquiry service provides general information and guidance on all aspects of building as well as product information.

Construction Resources
16 Great Guildford Street
London SE1 0HS
020 7450 2211
www.constructionresources.com
Britain's first ecological building centre, for advice and suppliers.

The Federation of Master Builders
14–15 Great James Street
London WC1N 3DP
020 7242 7583
www.fmb.org.uk
Represents small and medium-sized building firms and issues a membership card to member tradespeople. Visit their website to find a builder.

The Institution of Structural Engineers
11 Upper Belgrave Street
London SW1X 8BH
020 7235 4535
www.istructe.org
The Institution publishes a Yearbook of Members and a Directory of Firms for the UK and can put you in touch with a structural engineer in your area.

Royal Institute of British Architects
Clients' Advisory Service
66 Portland Place
London W1N 4AD
020 7307 3700
www.riba.org
The RIBA Clients' Advisory Service and can put you in touch with an RIBA registered architect who practices in your area. (n.b. Not all qualified architects register with the RIBA).

The Royal Institution of Chartered Surveyors
12 Great George Street
London SW1P 3AD
020 7222 7000
www.rics.org
The RICS will supply details of qualified members in your area.

FLOORING

Dalsouple
01278 727 733
www.dalsouple.com
Rubber flooring tiles in a multitude of different colours and designs.

Gooding Aluminium
1 British Wharf
Landmann Way
London SE14 5RS
020 8692 2255
www.goodingalum.com
Sheet aluminium flooring, walls and stair treads in a variety of designs.

Delabole Slate
Pengelly Road
Delabole
Cornwall PL33 9AZ
01840 212 242
www.delabole.co.uk
Slate slabs for flooring, worksurfaces and fireplaces.

The Hardwood Flooring Co. Ltd
31-35 Fortune Green Road
London NW6 1DU
020 7431 7000
www.hardwoodflooringcompany.com
Large selection of wood flooring.

Stone Age
Unit 3
Parsons Green Depot
Parsons Green Lane
London SW6 4HH
www.estone.co.uk
Over 40 types of limestone and sandstone.

KITCHENS

Bulthaup
37 Wigmore Street
London W1U 1PP
020 7495 3663
www.bulthaup.co.uk
Streamlined modern kitchens with excellent lighting and storage.

IKEA
2 Drury Way
London NW10 0TH
020 8208 5600
Visit www.ikea.co.uk for details of their other stores.
Inexpensive modern flat-packed self-assembly kitchens.

Pages
121 Shaftesbury Avenue
London WC2H 8AD
020 7565 5959
www.pagescatering.co.uk
Professional catering equipment and accessories.

Kay + Stemmer
Oblique Workshops
Stamford Works
Gillett Street
London N16 8JH
020 7503 2105
www.kay-stemmer.co.uk
Andrea Stemmer's 'one-unit' stainless steel kitchens in custom-built oak and glass cabinets are ideal for small open-plan homes.

John Strand
12-22 Herga Road
Wealdstone
Harrow
Middlesex HA3 5AS
020 8930 6006
www.johnstrand-mk.co.uk
*A wide range of mini-kitchens
for small spaces.*

DIVIDERS

Armourcoat Limited
Morewood Close
London Road
Sevenoaks
Kent TN13 2HU
01732 460 668
www.armourcoat.com
*Suppliers of unique polished
hard plaster wall finishes that
can be sealed and made
waterproof.*

Connections Interiors Ltd
286-288 Leigh Road
Leigh on Sea
Essex SS9 1BW
01702 470 909
Mobile partitioning and screens.

Ergonom
Whittington House
19–30 Alfred House
London WC1E 7EA
020 7323 2325
www.ergonom.com
*Glazed and solid screens and
moving partitions.*

ICI
Telephone 01254 874000 for
details and stockists
www.ici.com
*Manufacturers of a wide range
of perspex, which can be used
for mobile screens, partitions,
doors, flooring and surfaces.*

Luxcrete
Premier House
Disraeli Road
London NW10 7BT
020 8965 7292
www.luxcrete.co.uk
*Glass blocks in a range of
different sizes and patterns, for
commercial and domestic use.*

Space Slide
Portico Limited
Middlemore Lane
Aldridge, Walsall
West Midlands WS9 8SP
01922 743211
www.spaceslide.co.uk
*Contemporary room dividers and
sliding walls.*

Spazio
01580 763593
www.spazio.co.uk
*Custom-made folding glass and
aluminium doors, walls and
room dividers.*

LIGHTING

John Cullen Lighting
585 Kings Road
London SW6 2EH
020 7371 5400
www.johncullenlighting.co.uk
*Made-to-measure lighting design
for both house and garden.*

London Lighting Company
135 Fulham Road
London SW3 6 RT
020 7589 3612
www.londonlighting.co.uk
*Wonderful selection of
contemporary lighting.*

SKK
34 Lexington Street
London W1R 3HR
020 7434 4095
www.skk.net
*Architectural lighting and
cutting-edge lighting designers.*

STORAGE

The Holding Company
243–245 Kings Road
London SW3 5EL
020 7352 1600
www.theholdingcompany.co.uk
*Comprehensive range of
predominantly small-scale
storage ideas.Good for clothing
and shoe storage.*

Muji
35 Long Acre
London WC2E 9AD.
020 7379 0820
Visit www.muji.co.uk for details
of their other stores.
*Large range of inexpensive but
stylish minimalist storage.*

FURNITURE

Century
68 Marylebone High Street
London W1U 5HJ
020 7487 5100
*Contemporary classic furniture,
predominantly 20th-century
American designs.*

Coexistence
288 Upper Street
London N1 2TZ
020 7354 8817
www.coexistence.co.uk
*A comprehensive collection of
contemporary European
furniture.*

The Conran Shop
81 Fulham Road
London SW3 6RD
020 7589 7401
www.conran.com
*One-stop shopping for
contemporary furniture, lighting,
bed linen, kitchen equipment
and accessories.*

Purves & Purves
www.purves.co.uk
*Modern furniture, lighting and
accessories.*

SCP
135–139 Curtain Road
London EC2A 3BX
020 7739 1869
www.scp.co.uk
*Contemporary European
furniture and lighting in one of
the most exciting showrooms in
London.*

twentytwentyone
274 Upper Street
London N1 2UA
020 7288 1996
www.twentytwentyone.com
*Inspiring collection of mid-
century classics.*

Viaduct
1–10 Summer's Street
London EC1R 5BD
020 7278 8456
www.viaduct.co.uk
*Comprehensive selection of
European furniture and lighting
in an exciting showroom.*

Vitra
30 Clerkenwell Road
London EC1M 5QP
020 7608 6200
www.vitra.com
Contemporary furniture.

business credits

**ARCHITECTS AND DESIGNERS
WHOSE WORK HAS BEEN
FEATURED IN THIS BOOK**

Babylon Design Ltd
Lighting designers
301 Fulham Road
London SW10 9QH
020 7376 7233
www.babylonlondon.com
Pages 14, 23, 100–101, 125 right

Claire Bataille & Paul ibens
Vekestraat 13 Bus 14
2000 Antwerpen
Belgium
+32 3 213 86 20
www.bataille-ibens.be
*Pages 1 centre, 3, 18, 40–45,
121 left, 129 top left*

Briffa Phillips
19-21 Holywell Hill
St Albans, Herts AL1 1EZ
01727 840 567
www.briffaphillips.com
*Pages 26 top, 26-27, 62-63, 82,
83 top left and below left*

Brookes Stacey Randall
For this project :
Space Craft Architects
16 Winchester Walk
London SE1 9AQ

020 7407 9394
www.spacecraft-architects.com
*Pages 1 right, 32-33, 68-69,
112-113, 116 below both, 117
right, 127 top*

**dMFK (de Metz Forbes Knight
Architects), formerly de Metz
Architects**
Unit 4, 250 Finchley Road
London NW3 6DN
020 7435 1144
www.dmfk.co.uk
*Pages 15 left and right, 92 all,
130 right*

**Jamie Falla
MooArc**
198 Blackstock Road
London N5 1EN
020 7354 1729
www.mooarc.com
*Pages 26 below, 48 and 49 left,
66-67, 87 both*

Han Feng
Fashion designer
333 West 39 Street, 12th floor
New York, NY 10018
001 212 695 9509
www.hanfeng.com
*Pages 16, 31 right, 50–51,
84–85, 88–89, 115 top right,
136 top left*

**Fernlund and Logan
Architects**
414 Broadway
New York, NY 10013
001 212 925 9628
www.fernlundlogan.com
*Pages 7 right, 12–13, 46–47,
54–55, 116–117 centre, 135 left*

Alastair Hendy
Food writer, art director and
designer
www.alastairhendy.com
*Pages 4, 10–11, 34 left, 72–79,
102 below right, 120, 123 right,
125 left, 130 centre, 131 left,
135 centre, 136 below left, 144
centre*

**Brian Johnson
Johnson Naylor**
020 7490 8885
www.johnsonnaylor.co.uk
*Pages 2, 26 below, 56–61, 122
centre, 134, 144 right*

Steven Learner Studio
307 Seventh Avenue Room 2201
New York, NY 10001
001 212 741 8583
www.stevenlearnerstudio.com
*Pages 52–53, 80–81, 116 top
left, 123 left*

Littman Goddard Hogarth
61 Courtfield Gardens
London SW5 0NQ
020 7565 8366
www.hogartharchitects.co.uk
*Pages 71, 86 all, 93, 102 below
left, 126, 128 below, 129 below
left, 144 left*

LOT/EK Architecture
55 Little West 12th Street
New York, NY 10014
001 212 255 9326
www.lot-ek.com
Pages 28, 29 left, 106–111

Marino + Giolito
161 West 16th Street
New York, NY 10011
001 212 675 5737
marino.giolito@rcn.com
Pages 104–105, 129 right

Orefelt Associates
43 Pall Mall Deposit
124-128 Barlby Road
London
W10 6BL
t. 020 8960 2560
*Pages 6, 24, 34 right, 102 top
right, 103,*

Architeam Ltd
Campfield House
Powdermill Lane
Battle
East Sussex TN33 0SY
01424 775211
www.architeam.co.uk
*Pages 25 top right, 35, 64 right,
65 all, 121 centre and right, 122
right, 131 centre*

Evelyn Roussel
00 33 1 43 55 76 97
*Pages 20–21, 118–119, 135
right*

**Stickland Coombe
Architecture**
258 Lavender Hill
London SW11 1LJ
020 7924 1699
*Endpapers, pages 8–9, 124, 128
top, 130 left*

Totem Design Group
71 Franklin Street
New York, NY 10013
001 212 925 5506
Fax: 001 212 925 5082
www.totemdesign.com
*Pages 22, 114–115 main and
top left and centre*

Urban Salon Ltd
Unit D
Flat Iron Yard
Ayres Street
London SE1 1ES
020 7357 8800
www.urbansalonarchitects.com
Pages 70 both, 131 right

Woolf Architects
27 Swinton Street
London WC1X 9NW
020 7692 1086
*Pages 5,19, 30, 30–31 centre,
64 top left and below left, 90
below right, 91, 132–133*

picture credits

Key: t = top, b = below, l = left, r = right, c = centre

1 l Gabriele Sanders' apartment in New York; 1 c an apartment in Knokke, Belgium designed by Claire Bataille and Paul ibens; 1 r Nik Randall, Suzsi Corio and Louis' home in London designed by Brookes Stacey Randall; 2 Brian Johnson's apartment in London designed by Johnson Naylor; 3 an apartment in Knokke, Belgium designed by Claire Bataille and Paul ibens; 4 Alastair Hendy & John Clinch's apartment in London designed by Alastair Hendy; 5 Patricia Ijaz's house in London designed by Jonathan Woolf of Woolf Architects; 6 a house in London designed by Orefelt Associates, Design team Gunnar Orefelt and Knut Hovland; 7 l Nik Randall, Suzsi Corio and Louis' home in London designed by Brookes Stacey Randall; 7 r Jeff Priess and Rebecca Quaytman's apartment in New York designed by Fernlund and Logan Architects, painting by Rebecca Quaytman; 8–9 Anthony Swanson's apartment in London designed by Stickland Coombe Architecture; 10–11 Alastair Hendy & John Clinch's apartment in London designed by Alastair Hendy; 12–13 Jeff Priess and Rebecca Quaytman's apartment in New York designed by Fernlund and Logan Architects; 14 Babylon Design Studio in London Ltd.; 15 Nicki De Metz's flat in London designed by De Metz architects; 16 Han Feng's apartment in New York designed by Han Feng; 17 Christian Baquiast's apartment in Paris; 18 an apartment in Knokke, Belgium designed by Claire Bataille and Paul ibens; 19 Patricia Ijaz's house in London designed by Jonathan Woolf; 20–21 Evelyne Rousell's apartment in Paris; 22 David Shearer and Gail Schultz's apartment in New York; 23 Babylon Design Ltd. studio in London; 24 a house in London designed by Orefelt Associates, Design team Gunnar Orefelt and Knut Hovland; 25 t Andrew Noble's apartment in London designed by Nico Rensch Architeam; 25 b Jamie Falla and Lynn Graham's house in London; 26 t an apartment in Bath designed by Briffa Phillips Architects; 26 b Brian Johnson's apartment in London designed by

Johnson Naylor; 26–27 an apartment in Bath designed by Briffa Phillips Architects; 28 & 29 l Jones Miller studio in New York designed by Giuseppe Lignano and Ada Tolla of LOT/EK Architecture; 29 r Christian Baquiast's apartment in Paris; 30 l & 30–31 c Patricia Ijaz's house in London designed by Jonathan Woolf; 31 r Han Feng's apartment in New York designed by Han Feng; 32–33 Nik Randall, Suzsi Corio and Louis' home in London designed by Brookes Stacey Randall; 34 l Alastair Hendy & John Clinch's apartment in London designed by Alastair Hendy; 34 r a house in London designed by Orefelt Associates, Design team Gunnar Orefelt and Knut Hovland; 35 Andrew Noble's apartment in London designed by Nico Rensch Architeam; 36–37 Gabriele Sanders' apartment in New York; 38 Christian Baquiast's apartment in Paris; 39 Christian Baquiast's apartment in Paris; 41–45 an apartment in Knokke, Belgium designed by Claire Bataille and Paul ibens; 46–47 Jeff Priess and Rebecca Quaytman's apartment in New York designed by Fernlund and Logan Architects; 48 & 49 l Jamie Falla and Lynn Graham's house in London; 50–51 Han Feng's apartment in New York designed by Han Feng; 52–53 the loft of Peggy and Steven Learner designed by Steven Learner Studio; 54–55 Jeff Priess and Rebecca Quaytman's apartment in New York designed by Fernlund and Logan Architects; 56–61 Brian Johnson's apartment in London designed by Johnson Naylor; 62–63 an apartment in Bath designed by Briffa Phillips Architects; 64 tl & bl Patricia Ijaz's house in London designed by Jonathan Woolf of Woolf Architects; 64 r & 65 Andrew Noble's apartment in London designed by Nico Rensch Architeam; 66–67 Jamie Falla and Lynn Graham's house in London; 68–69 Nik Randall, Suzsi Corio and Louis' home in London designed by Brookes Stacey Randall; 70 both Lucy Guard's apartment in London designed by Urban Salon; 71 an apartment in London designed by Littman Goddard Hogarth Architects; 72–79 Alastair Hendy & John Clinch's apartment in London designed by Alastair Hendy; 80–81 the loft of Peggy and Steven Learner designed by Steven Learner Studio; 82-83 an

apartment in Bath designed by Briffa Phillips Architects; 84–85 Han Feng's apartment in New York designed by Han Feng; 86 an apartment in London designed by Littman Goddard Hogarth Architects; 87 Jamie Falla and Lynn Graham's house in London; 88–89 Han Feng's apartment in New York designed by Han Feng; 90 tl & tr Christian Baquiast's apartment in Paris; 90 br & 91 Patricia Ijaz's house in London designed by Jonathan Woolf of Woolf Architects; 92 Nicki De Metz's flat in London designed by De Metz architects; 93 an apartment in London designed by Littman Goddard Hogarth Architects; 94–99 Gabriele Sanders' apartment in New York, 99 chairs from Totem; 100–101 Babylon Design Ltd. studio in London; 102 bl an apartment in London designed by Littman Goddard Hogarth Architects; 102br Alastair Hendy & John Clinch's apartment in London designed by Alastair Hendy; 102 tr & 103 a house in London designed by Orefelt Associates, Design team Gunnar Orefelt and Knut Hovland; 104–105 Chelsea Studio New York City, designed by Marino and Giolito; 106–111 Jones Miller studio in New York designed by Giuseppe Lignano and Ada Tolla of LOT/EK Architecture; 112–113 Nik Randall, Suzsi Corio and Louis' home in London designed by Brookes Stacey Randall; 114 & inset & 115 c David Shearer and Gail Schultz's apartment in New York; 115 tr Han Feng's apartment in New York designed by Han Feng; 116 tl the loft of Peggy and Steven Learner designed Steven Learner Studio; 116 b both Nik Randall, Suzsi Corio and Louis' home in London designed by Brookes Stacey Randall; 116–117 c Jeff Priess and Rebecca Quaytman's apartment in New York designed by Fernlund and Logan Architects; 117 r Nik Randall, Suzsi Corio and Louis' home in London designed by Brookes Stacey Randall; 118–119 Evelyn Rousell's apartment in Paris; 120 Alastair Hendy & John Clinch's apartment in London designed by Alastair Hendy; 121 l an apartment in Knokke, Belgium designed by Claire Bataille and Paul ibens; 121 c & r Andrew Noble's apartment in London designed by Nico Rensch Architeam; 122 l Nello Renault's loft in Paris; 122 c Brian Johnson's apartment in London designed by Johnson Naylor; 122 r Andrew Noble's apartment in London designed by Nico Rensch

Architeam; 123 l the loft of Peggy and Steven Learner designed by Steven Learner Studio; 123 r Alastair Hendy & John Clinch's apartment in London designed by Alastair Hendy; 124 Anthony Swanson's apartment in London designed by Stickland Coombe Architecture; 125 l Alastair Hendy & John Clinch's apartment in London designed by Alastair Hendy; 125 r Babylon Design Ltd. studio in London; 126 an apartment in London designed by Littman Goddard Hogarth Architects; 127 t Nik Randall, Suzsi Corio and Louis' home in London designed by Brookes Stacey Randall; 127 b Christian Baquiast's apartment in Paris; 128 t Anthony Swanson's apartment in London designed by Stickland Coombe Architecture; 128 b & 129 bl an apartment in London designed by Littman Goddard Hogarth Architects; 129 tl an apartment in Knokke, Belgium designed by Claire Bataille and Paul ibens; 129 r Chelsea Studio New York City, designed by Marino and Giolito; 130 l Anthony Swanson's apartment in London designed by Stickland Coombe Architecture; 130 c & 131 l Alastair Hendy & John Clinch's apartment in London designed by Alastair Hendy; 130 r Nicki De Metz's flat in London designed by De Metz architects; 131 c Andrew Noble's apartment in London designed by Nico Rensch Architeam; 131 r Lucy Guard's apartment in London designed by Urban Salon; 132–133 Patricia Ijaz's house in London designed by Jonathan Woolf of Woolf Architects; 134 Brian Johnson's apartment in London designed by Johnson Naylor; 135 l Jeff Priess and Rebecca Quaytman's apartment in New York designed by Fernlund and Logan Architects; 135 c Alastair Hendy & John Clinch's apartment in London designed by Alastair Hendy; 135 r Evelyne Roussel's house in Paris; 136 tl Han Feng's apartment in New York designed by Han Feng; 136 b Alastair Hendy & John Clinch's apartment in London designed by Alastair Hendy; 140 Gabriele Sanders' apartment in New York; 144 l an apartment in London designed by Littman Goddard Hogarth Architects; 144 c Alastair Hendy & John Clinch's apartment in London designed by Alastair Hendy; 144 r Brian Johnson's apartment in London designed by Johnson Naylor.

index

Figures in italics refer to captions.

acknowledgements

Thank you Andrew Wood, for your great pictures and your appetite for photography, interiors, people, travel and sushi. Thank you everyone at Ryland Peters & Small, for presenting me with this opportunity. Thank you Anne Ryland, Kate Brunt, Megan Smith and Annabel Morgan – in the order I first met you – for your commitment and interest in this project; your individual and professional input is evident in the book. Thank you Nadine Bazar, for your essential contribution.

My biggest thanks to everyone living in a single space who said yes to photography and to all the architects and designers whose work is included. Thank you all for your hospitality, inspiration, imagination and originality. Thank you to everyone who gave me their valuable time and helpful information and suggestions.

Finally, thank you Lawrence Morton. And thank you Atom. Although I long to live in several places in this book, my home is the people I live with.